HERE TOMORROW

HERE TOMORROW

PRESERVING ARCHITECTURE, CULTURE, AND CALIFORNIA'S GOLDEN DREAMS

J. K. Dineen

Foreword by John King

Heyday, Berkeley, California

Special thanks for support of this book to Cahill Contractors, Inc., Charles Edwin Chase AIA, Historic Resources Group, Steve Hearst, and Cindy Heitzman.

The publisher has made every reasonable attempt to contact and secure reprint permission from photographers, architecture firms, and other sources for the photographs reproduced in this book. If you have any additional information about photography sources and credits, we would be grateful to hear about it: www.heydaybooks.com.

Cover Art: Ennis House, image © Ron Luxemburg
Cover Design: Lorraine Rath
Interior Design/Typesetting: Rebecca LeGates
Image Editor: Karen Sorensen

Library of Congress Cataloging-in-Publication Data
Dineen, J. K. (John Kelley), 1968-
  Here tomorrow : preserving architecture, culture, and California's golden dreams / J.K. Dineen ; foreword by John King.
    pages cm
  ISBN 978-1-59714-236-6 (hardcover : alk. paper)
  1. Architecture--Conservation and restoration--California.
  2. Historic sites--Conservation and restoration--California. I. Title.
  NA107.C3D56 2013
  720.9794--dc23
                                        2013007368

Orders, inquiries, and correspondence should be addressed to:
    Heyday
    P.O. Box 9145, Berkeley, CA 94709
    (510) 549-3564, Fax (510) 549-1889
    www.heydaybooks.com

Printed in China by Everbest Printing Co. through Four Colour Imports, Ltd., Louisville, KY

10 9 8 7 6 5 4 3 2 1

CONTENTS

FOREWORD

John King

HERE TOMORROW: *Preserving Architecture, Culture, and California's Golden Dreams* is, on the surface, a well-illustrated collection that presents the stories behind the rehabilitation and revitalization of fifty historic properties—a garden and an aircraft carrier among the more conventional kinds of buildings you'd expect—in the decades since the California Preservation Foundation was founded in 1978 to, in the words of the group's original mission statement, "ensure that California's rich and diverse historic resources are identified, protected, and celebrated." But the thread that links these case studies isn't the architectural history of the state, or the technical expertise required to turn back the clock and nurture frail buildings to health. It is something more subtle and resonant than that: the importance of individuals like you and me to the landscape we share.

The preservation movement, after all, long ago moved beyond the (arguably) elitist roots that critics still disparage today. Preservationism took hold in the 1960s because of a realization that if America's built terrain was left to fend for itself, then many of our culture's most important shared landmarks would disappear. These older structures were obsolete in the eyes of developers and decision makers: too small or too much trouble, in need of too much work, in the path of

change, or out of official favor with regard to the purpose they served and the way they looked.

There's nothing inherently evil about the fact that this nation grew and prospered by building up and tearing down, or that we continue to do so today. But as the pace of change accelerated after World War II, so did the perils of business as usual. People were confronted with what was at risk: the gathering spots that span generations, the impossible-to-replicate gems, the everyday structures that by their presence offer clues to how we came to be what we are. California was not spared in this rush to raze; quite the contrast. By the time politicians extolled a population boom that in December of 1962 made this the most populous state, every big city and small town had its own horror stories of touchstones lost. People from all walks of life were learning firsthand the value of things taken for granted until they are gone, and as the shock wore off, those citizens responded—first by rallying around obvious treasures, and then by seeking to cast protective nets around entire neighborhoods or buildings that stirred affection even if the architectural pedigree was thin.

In the decades since then, we have lost many battles but won many more. In many California communities, the reuse of existing buildings has become, rightly so, the starting point of any discussion about the evolution of the landscape. We've learned the virtues of context. Not all properties will be saved—and I hope the most ardent preservationists won't be horrified if I suggest that not all should be—but even development boosters are now forced to concede the value of holding on to physical, palpable links to the past.

Factors larger than any lone advocate have aided the cause as well.

Seismic upheaval, for instance. Earthquakes are the Golden State's ominous given, and after the 1989 Loma Prieta and 1994 Northridge temblors, building owners were prodded by circumstances to repair or upgrade (often helped by federal and state disaster-relief funding that would not have been available otherwise) aged treasures that otherwise might have languished. The payoff was visible for all to see—and the good feelings generated by those investments helped convince neighbors and other municipalities to attempt the same rejuvenation of their own faded gems.

Similarly, the public affection for such old-becomes-new spaces as festival marketplaces predates the California Preservation Foundation—think back to the sensation caused by Ghirardelli Square and the Cannery in 1960s San Francisco—but it has been validated again and again. And when the marketplace confirms the added value of historic ambiance, profit-seeking developers take notice.

In the process of this journey we have learned something else, as this book shows: the desire to save takes us only so far. The future of the past often requires leaps of imagination, whether the challenge is to find an economic rationale for rehabilitation or to rebuff earthquakes with no visible effort. This is where individuals

figure in as well—architects, engineers, crusaders and craftspeople—because without their creative passion, too many good intentions would fall short.

The ingenuity of such individuals is the aspect of historical preservation, adaptation, and interpretation that makes California's triumphs so instructive. As people have worked to save the buildings and landscapes that their communities hold dear, the paths they have taken to achieve that goal are as varied as can be.

SOME OF THE CASE STUDIES that follow are straightforward sagas of care lavished on a tarnished but deserving jewel, such as the Kaufmann House in Palm Springs, designed in 1946 by Richard Neutra—the personification of one chic aspect of the California Dream, yet demeaned by a generation of faddish alterations until it was fastidiously restored in the 1990s by new owners. The happy ending can also spring from the arrival of a single benefactor with a good heart and deep pockets: Wallis Annenberg explained her donation of $27.5 million to restore a publicly owned Santa Monica pool and guesthouse, built as part of an estate for William Randolph Hearst, by saying "this glorious expanse of sea and sand, this stunning vista, should belong to us all."

These two stories play into the conventional narrative of preservation as a rich person's pursuit. But then we read of Friendship Baptist Church in Pasadena, a Spanish Revival church closed after damage from the Northridge earthquake, then revived and brought up to code by worshipers who would not let it go. Today the church is home to a largely African American congregation, and also used to provide shelter for homeless families. And there's the tough love that jolted Globe

Mills in Sacramento back to life after forty dormant years. Construction workers turned flour silos into elevator shafts and residential spaces, even sawing window openings into eight-inch-thick concrete as part of a successful effort to make room for 114 low-income senior apartments—a particularly striking example of how buildings across the state have taken on a new purpose: providing shelter for people with few other options.

The buildings and structures themselves in this book are as diverse as the tales of how they came to be saved. Anyone who cares about California architecture knows San Francisco City Hall, designed by Bakewell and Brown and topped by a 307-foot-tall dome that now includes a $500,000 gold-leaf finish added as part of a wondrous post–Loma Prieta makeover. But few of us know Mendocino's Temple of Kwan Tai, which has endured since the 1850s despite consisting of little more than two doors, three windows, and wooden walls painted bright green and red. Some buildings have designs that could be found nowhere else, like Frank Lloyd Wright's Ennis House, with its craggy Mayan air of make-believe above Los Angeles. Others were once commonplace, such as the thirteen workers' cottages in Hercules that housed employees of a dynamite factory. But then, when the factory town became a suburb, the cottages were moved and reborn as starter homes that double as the sole trace of architectural history in an era of tract homes and shopping centers.

Then there are popular icons that defy classification—of which no better example is found within these pages than the LAX Theme Building. Its eye-catching collision of four 135-foot-high parabolic steel arches, designed by Pereira & Luckman, sprang skyward in 1961 and "made the statement that L.A. was more about where it was going than where it had been," in J. K. Dineen's apt phrase. Now it has been made seismically safe by an audacious sleight of hand: a 1.2 million-pound weight hidden in the summit where the four arches meet, anchoring them safely into place but keeping the aura of sci-fi whimsy intact.

For every building that is restored and continues on as before, another one flourishes in a far different role than its creators could ever have conceived, as with Globe Mills's delayed second act. For every building that gets a second chance through conventional means—that is, a developer doing a development project—another is saved by volunteers laboring out of sheer love on their own time and at their own pace as resources allow. Without such devotion, the Point Sur Lighthouse surely would be dark today.

The act of preservation can be an act of civic affirmation, as when the long-troubled city of Richmond, on the shores of San Francisco Bay, restored and modernized its 1940s Civic Center to once again house its municipal government and, if all goes well, to help revive its faded downtown core. Preservation can also be an act of penance. California has an example of this in Manzanar Guard Tower #8, rebuilt at the site of a Japanese American internment camp in Inyo County, forty years after it was torn down with the rest of the camp and sold for scrap.

ULTIMATELY, THE MESSAGE OF this book is that our culture cannot, and should not, separate the new from the old.

In a very real sense, the buildings around us embody California's sense of itself. They show what was aspired to and, at a more prosaic level, what this or that generation expected from the structures in which people lived their everyday lives. Then, after the initial glow fades, the buildings that survive bear testimony to how we regard our past. When they're left to decay or languish, as was the interim fate of too many buildings in this book, the implicit message is that our society either doesn't have the ability to safeguard its inheritance or simply doesn't care.

Buildings do not exist in isolation, each structure unto itself, for the built landscape in turn shapes the future—heights to be exceeded, standards to be maintained, mistakes to avoid. (Freeways connecting regions? Good. Freeways severing neighborhoods? Bad.) Buildings are frames of reference. By being able to explore the actual spaces, to see and touch the structural layers, we're more informed about how that landscape can be improved on as, inevitably, more changes come our way. This also is why the preservation of archeological sites and historical settings is so important, every bit as much as the preservation of buildings.

Take away that heritage, or let it fade in moribund neglect, and a society loses its mooring. But preservationists are smarter than that. By saving and then reviving strands in the urban fabric around us, they demonstrate that buildings can evolve as surely as the populations that pass through them. Technological innovations can serve the cause of architectural conservation. Second acts exist.

One small final lesson from *Here Tomorrow* is that the definition of what constitutes a "landmark" will never be resolved. This is an expansive age; the days are gone when buildings only deserved saving if George Washington Slept Here or if they were the architectural equivalent of Best in Show. Treasures such as the Temple of Kwan Tai or the workers' homes of Hercules are cultural relics, of historical merit for their everyday significance; they show us how things once were. With each decade or generation that passes, "the past" grows ever more varied and complex. As more layers of experience accumulate on our landscape, perceptive Californians will continue to see new value in structural types and styles that otherwise would be torn down or left to rot.

The story of historic preservation in California is only just getting started. The book in your hands shows that it already has left an invaluable mark.

ACKNOWLEDGMENTS

THIS BOOK WOULD NOT have been possible without the California Preservation Foundation and its irrepressible members who fight every day to save worthy historic structures across the state.

CPF Executive Director Cindy Heitzman not only helped shape the book but also gave me a tour of wine-industry landmarks in St. Helena, a town where she spent ten years as the building official and fire marshal. CPF interns Anita Y. Wu and Sang Bae provided valuable research assistance. Many CPF board members—past and present—were also instrumental. Steade Craigo, retired from the California State Office of Historic Preservation, was one such board alumnus. In Pasadena, I benefited from the encyclopedic knowledge of Peyton Hall, Christy McAvoy, and Andrea Humberger of the Historic Resources Group. At Page & Turnbull in San Francisco, preservation legend Jay Turnbull provided deep background on several projects, as did Carolyn Kiernat and John Lesak. The folks at Architectural Resources Group patiently guided me through a roster of projects, and I am indebted to Stephen Farneth, Naomi Miroglio, Charles Chase, and David Wassel. In San Diego I would have been completely lost without Ione Stiegler of IS Architecture, who chauffered me around while illuminating county history.

Urban design guru John King of the *San Francisco Chronicle* was kind enough to recommend me to Heyday. *San Francisco Business Times* editors Steve Symanovich and Jim Gardner believed in the project and indulged me with time off when I needed it, as did publisher Mary Huss. Many friends provided editorial guidance, and in some cases helped with child care, including: Ethan Fletcher, Jay Brida, Nick Driver, Paul Buddenhagen, Paul Harding, Nina Fletcher, Cindy Chew, Mark Triplett, Shara Mays, Michael Andrews, Josie Laine Andrews, and the late Jonathan Kuperman. As did my sisters, Jane, Martha, Louisa, and Jessica; and my father, John K. Dineen.

One of my favorite parts of doing this project was the chance to work with Heyday, a magical Berkeley institution that truly could only exist in California.

Heyday founder Malcolm Margolin (a fellow Boston refugee) told me to have fun with it and make it my own. Gayle Wattawa and Marilee Enge are sharp editors and kept me grounded and on course (no easy feat).

Finally, this book is dedicated to my wife, Megan Fletcher, and children, Amelia Rose Dineen and Patrick Hemenway Dineen. They saw a lot less of me while I was exploring sites or off writing at cafes and libraries. I hope this book will provide color and texture as we explore the back roads and downtowns of our adopted home state.

ONLY IN CALIFORNIA

Some places are hard to imagine taking root outside of California. A Hollywood set designer builds a fantasy Swiss chalet in the desert and turns it into a museum of Native American artifacts. A Chinese American family fights to protect a Buddhist temple on the rugged Mendocino hillside long after the local Chinese American community has vanished. In Glendale, volunteers rally to save an atmospherium theater where Hollywood stars once snuck in to watch screenings of their own films.

LAX Theme Building, Image © Vince Tanzilli, Miyamoto International.

MILLS COLLEGE MUSIC BUILDING OAKLAND

DID THE BUILDING make the music or the music make the building?

For more than a century, one of the country's most important contemporary music programs has operated in relative obscurity at Oakland's Mills College. In the 1930s the Pro Arte String Quartet took up residence there, performing American premieres of works by Stravinsky and Bartók. Jazz innovator Dave Brubeck showed up in 1946, fresh from the army, learning polytonality from French composer Darius Milhaud. Electronic music pioneer Morton Subotnick studied at Mills, as did performance artist Laurie Anderson, Grateful Dead bassist Phil Lesh, and computer music pioneer Leland Smith. Freak folkster Joanna Newsom plucked her harp

Above: The rehabilitated lobby features new niches with cast-stone benches under original stone lintels, a reinforced and beautifully refinished cast-plaster ceiling, and a floor that mixes salvaged clay tiles with new ones. *Opposite:* Main entrance after rehabilitation. *Previous page:* The new walls of the Jeannik Méquet Littlefield Concert Hall feature an elegant system of reflective and absorptive panels to distribute sound. All images © 2008 Cesar Rubio.

there; minimalist Steve Reich left Julliard for Mills in 1961, although he later found it "boring and frustrating."

As improbable as Mills's contribution to music was, so too was the building in which it flourished. In the 1920s Mills College Architect Walter Ratcliff joined forces with Depression-era muralist Raymond Boynton to create a 450-seat performance hall with a "scheme of decoration which would give free play to the imagination." The building mixes Baroque ornamentation with California whimsy. Ornate wrought-iron-and-mica chandeliers illuminate Boynton's gold-and-pastel choir-loft murals depicting the California landscape.

But over the decades the concert hall started to decay. Termites lunched on the hall's Celotex acoustic panels, which are made from sugarcane residue. Water-damaged walls were coated with waterproofing that lent them a moldy pea-green hue. The six fres-

coes depicting scenes from classical mythology faded. The hand-painted geometric ceiling tiles were falling apart. "It was like ancient Rome in here," said current Mills College Architect Karen Fiene.

And then there was the noise. Music faculty member David Bernstein remembers the night in 1995 when composer Maggi Payne was recording John Cage's *Sonatas and Interludes* at the school concert hall. The piece, the sixteen sonatas and four interludes, was going beautifully. Except for one little matter: every few minutes a jet from Oakland International Airport roared overhead. "She had to stop and wait for airplanes to go by and then try again; it happened over and over and over," said Bernstein.

An eighteen-month, $11 million renovation finished in 2009 enclosed the auditorium with a massive roof that blocked out external noises. Eight decades

Detail of the carved stone portal and bronze entrance after rehabilitation. Image © 2008 Cesar Rubio.

of dirt was removed from the artwork, and new wall panels were installed—basketweave-patterned acoustic tiles made of curved fiberglass wrapped in pearwood veneer. The building was seismically upgraded, and new lighting and sound systems were installed.

Named in honor of a noted Mills alumnus and patron of the arts, the Jeannik Méquet Littlefield Con-cert Hall reopened to the public in February 2009 with a six-concert series entitled Giving Free Play to the Imagination. "You walk past the place where so much history has unfolded and you feel the voices, you hear the voices," said Bernstein. "It's not just a little parochial school in California. It has that rich history and is not as well known as it should be."

BUILT: 1928

AWARDED: 2009

ORIGINAL ARCHITECT:
Walter Ratcliff

PRINCIPAL IN CHARGE: EHDD
Architecture, Jennifer Devlin

HISTORIC PRESERVATION
CONSULTANT: Architectural
Resources Group, Inc., Katharine
Untch, David Wessel, Kelly Wong,
and Lisa Kucik

STRUCTURAL ENGINEER:
Rutherford & Chekene, Dom
Campi

ART CONSERVATION:
Claire Antonetti Fine Art
Conservation, Claire Antonetti

FRESCO CONSERVATION:
Beau Art Studio, Barbara Bossak

GENERAL CONTRACTOR:
James R. Griffin, Inc., Randy
Griffin

ALEX THEATRE GLENDALE

FOR DECADES, Glendale's Alex Theatre played a vital supporting role in Hollywood: it was where studios tested their movies on what was considered a perfectly average suburban population. In 1944 Elizabeth Taylor watched the people of Glendale watching a preview of *National Velvet* at the Alex; a few months later Bing Crosby paced the lobby throughout the preview of *Going My Way*. "Movie stars were not supposed to attend their previews, but they often did," explained Andrea Humberger, a Glendale historian who spearheaded the Glendale Historical Society's effort to save the Alex. A half a century later, the community of Glendale proved

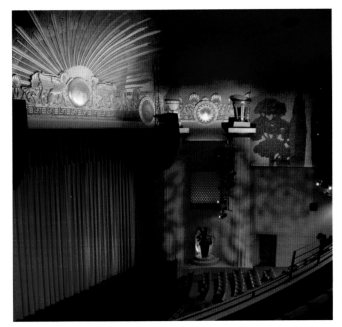

Above left: Image courtesy of Jessica Castillo, Glendale Arts. *Above right:* Image courtesy of Kate Shapiro, Glendale Arts. *Opposite and previous page:* Images © Randall Michelson/rmpix.com.

that when it came to saving California's endangered movie houses, it is anything but average.

The Alex, a Greek Revival theater with Egyptian motifs, was born in an era when movie houses were palaces—no theater could be too grand, no detail too exuberant. To enter into the Alex's auditorium, one of the few remaining atmospherium theaters in California, is to stroll into an ancient garden; 360-degree murals give theatergoers the illusion of being outside amid flowers, vines, and statues of gods.

The "beacon on Brand Boulevard" opened its doors on September 4, 1925, with John Ford's silent movie *Lightnin'* and eight vaudeville performances. Fifteen years later, theater architect S. Charles Lee upped the ante, adding the hundred-foot Art Deco neon column topped off by a neon "starburst." For years the theater was oper-

ated by Fox West Coast and then Mann Theatres, and it held its own until the late 1980s, when audiences drifted toward multiplexes with stadium seating.

But unlike so many other communities, the residents of Glendale refused to stand by and watch the landmark sit empty. In 1990, without even a solid plan for the theater, the city acquired a Fox Lanterman theater pipe organ from the city of La Cañada Flintridge for $50,000. In January of 1991 a task force made a list of recommendations for rehabilitation. At the time, Mayor Larry Zarian told the *Los Angeles Times:* "We are going to get a community theater that will make us all proud." A year later, the Glendale Redevelopment Agency invested $6.2 million to reinvent the theater as a performing-arts center. Humberger, a principal with Historic Resources Group, said it was notable how

Image © Randall Michelson/rmpix.com.

smoothly the advocacy effort to save the Alex went. "I don't know if we got lucky or the time was right or we were very convincing, but the city council just adopted the steps laid out by our theater consultants and systematically implemented them," she said.

Reopening on New Year's Eve 1993, the theater is today home to five resident companies: the Los Angeles Chamber Orchestra, the Gay Men's Chorus of Los Angeles, the Glendale Youth Orchestra, the Alex Film Society, and the Musical Theatre Guild. It is managed by Glendale Arts, a nonprofit organization. Some 250 events per year take place there, attended by 150,000 patrons. "The history of the Alex is that it has always been the center of the community. It's right in the middle of downtown. It has always paralleled what is going on in the city," said Humberger.

BUILT: 1925

AWARDED: 1991

ORIGINAL ARCHITECT:
Meyer & Holler

PRESERVATION ARCHITECT:
John Ash Group Architects

PROJECT MANAGER:
Wayne Ratkovich Company

GENERAL CONTRACTOR:
Turner Construction Company

STRUCTURAL ENGINEER:
Englekirk Structural Engineers

ANNENBERG COMMUNITY BEACH HOUSE
SANTA MONICA

THE FIRST TIME Santa Monica resident Lisa Robins plunged into the swimming pool at the Annenberg Community Beach House, she looked up at the sky and thought about those who had floated there before her: Charlie Chaplin, Winston Churchill, and, of course, the woman for whom the pool was built, silent-film star Marion Davies. It was hard to fathom that this was now a place where average citizens could pay a few bucks to spend the day with their kids.

The Annenberg Community Beach House is a public recreation complex built on one of California's most extraordinary stretches of beachfront property: 750 feet of frontage north of the Santa Monica Pier. It is a sun-drenched tapestry of new and old California that

Above: Image © Takashige Ikawa/Frederick Fisher and Partners, Architects. *Previous page:* Looking northeast at the new pool house, 2009. Image © Grant Mudford.

weaves the fabric of 1920s Gold Coast Santa Monica with the crisp eco-friendly minimalism of contemporary Los Angeles design.

Media mogul William Randolph Hearst developed the five-acre property in the 1920s for his companion, Marion Davies. The original Davies mansion, begun by William Flannery and completed by Julia Morgan, had thirty-five fireplaces, thirty-five bedrooms, and fifty-five bathrooms. Its ballroom came from a 1750 Venetian palazzo; its basement was an Elizabethan pub.

The parties Davies threw there drew Hollywood's most powerful figures, including Greta Garbo and Clark Gable. For a circus-themed party in 1937, Davies had a carousel transported from the Warner Brothers studio to her tennis courts.

During World War II, fearful of living so close to the water, Hearst and Davies relocated to San Simeon. In 1947 hotelier Joseph Drown bought the property and reinvented it as Ocean House, "America's Most Beautiful Hotel," and later as the Sand and Sea Club, a

Marion Davies Guest House. Image © Takashige Ikawa/Frederick Fisher and Partners, Architects.

private beach club. In 1958 Drown razed the main mansion with plans to erect a modern hotel. The hotel was never built, the State of California bought the property, and for the next thirty-three years it was a seasonal beach club and a set for TV shows like *Beverly Hills 90210*.

By the time the Northridge earthquake struck in 1994, only two original components of the property survived: a Julia Morgan–designed guesthouse and the famous swimming pool, with its marble deck and tropical-fish tiling. During the quake, a chimney col-

lapsed and crashed through the roof of the guesthouse, plummeting all the way to the first floor, but much of the original structure remained intact. A 1998 reuse plan called for the restoration of the guesthouse and pool, along with a new community beach house to be designed by Los Angeles architect Frederick Fisher.

The preservation architectural team, led by Peyton Hall of Historic Resources Group, went to great lengths to keep original wood siding, plaster, and floors—even where they were worn or nicked. The swimming pool, "[built] like a big concrete bathtub sitting in sand, had held up remarkably well," recalled Hall.

The design team wanted a clear distinction between the contemporary beach house and the historic pool and guesthouse. Fisher's beach house, with its fourteen concrete columns, pays tribute to the original mansion in form as well as its spatial relationship to the sea and guesthouse. But there is nothing classical about the building. It is made of concrete, cement board, wood, and glass. The very fabric of the building is sustainable, with insulation made of recycled blue jeans instead of fiberglass.

The beach house opened in April of 2009. At the grand opening, Los Angeles philanthropist Wallis Annenberg explained why she had provided $27.5 million for the project: "The truth is, this glorious expanse of sea and sand, this stunning vista, should belong to us all."

Community pool. Image © Takashige Ikawa/Frederick Fisher and Partners, Architects.

Historic pool and Marion Davies Guest House prior to restoration, 2004. Images courtesy of Frederick Fisher and Partners, Architects.

BUILT: 1920S

AWARDED: 2010

OWNER: California State Parks, Ron Schafer, District Superintendent

ORIGINAL ARCHITECT: William Flannery

PROJECT LEAD, FACILITY OPERATOR: City of Santa Monica

PROJECT ARCHITECT: Frederick Fisher and Partners, Architects, Frederick Fisher

HISTORIC PRESERVATION CONSULTANT: Historic Resources Group, Peyton Hall, FAIA

STRUCTURAL ENGINEER: KPFF Consulting Engineers, Joseph Stewart, SE

PROJECT MANAGER: Charles Pankow Builders, LLC, Rick Stupin

INTERIOR/EXTERIOR PRESERVATION & RESTORATION: Spectra Company, Ray Adamyk

HISTORIC PRESERVATION CONTRACTOR: Preservation Arts, Charles Kibby

LAX THEME BUILDING LOS ANGELES

IT WAS AN UNCONVENTIONAL approach to strengthening a building: construct a 1.2 million-pound steel weight and stick it up on the roof. But then again, the Theme Building at Los Angeles International Airport has never been a particularly conventional place.

Part of 1960's $50 million remodel of the airport, known as the "Los Angeles Jet Age Terminal Construc-

tion Project," the LAX Theme Building was completed in 1961. The building was designed to fill a hole. The original master plan for the 640-acre LAX, created by Pereira & Luckman in 1959, had called for a large glass dome in the geographical center of the airport, connecting terminals and parking garages. When the dome plan was abandoned, the design team, which included

Paul Williams and Welton Becket, had a prime piece of extraneous real estate on which to build a monument to the promise of the Jet Age.

The Theme Building did not disappoint. The design consisted of four 135-foot-high parabolic steel arches intersecting each other at ninety-degree angles. Was it a flying saucer perched on four spindly legs? Or did it look more like a white extraterrestrial spider wearing a sun visor? Either way, steeped in both the Populuxe and Googie design movements of the late 1950s and early 1960s, the nine-hundred-ton Jet Age structure made the statement that L.A. was more about where it was going than where it had been. It is hard to imagine city officials in Boston allotting public funds to plunk a giant UFO in the middle of Logan Airport.

With commercial aviation still in its infancy, the Theme Building's restaurant and observation deck immediately became a popular hangout for aircraft spotters. With the horizon to the west and downtown Los Angeles to the east, it was the perfect place to observe the latest the Boeing 707, Douglas DC-8, or Boeing 747 jets. "It's one of those wayfinder buildings that is printed on the consciousness of Los Angeles," said Linda Dishman, executive director of the Los Angeles Conservancy.

For thirty years the Theme Building remained more or less the same, although the restaurant went through a $4 million renovation in 1997 and reopened as the retro Jetson-themed Encounter Restaurant. A decade later, on February 24, 2007, a one-thousand-pound stucco

Above: Steel plates—1.2 million pounds of them in all—were craned above the Theme Building, one plate at a time, to strengthen the structure. Image courtesy of Miyamoto International. *Opposite:* Image © Vince Tanzilli, Miyamoto International.

slab fell from one of the upper arches and crashed into the structure's main platform, landing just feet from the restaurant. Nobody was hurt, but the crash inspectors discovered that rust had spread throughout the building's metal support system, likely caused by water that had leaked through its plaster seams. The discovery created a conundrum for the engineering team, led by Miyamoto International. How do you strengthen a building and make it earthquake-ready without screwing it up?

Rather than add lots of new concrete and steel, which would have been expensive and altered the building's look, the designers created a circular 1.2 million-pound steel weight that sits on eight flexible rubber bearings. Known as a tuned mass damper, it weighs as much as two 747s and anchors the existing roof of the central cylinder to the building. Essentially, it serves to counteract the movement of the structure in an earthquake. L. Scott Markle, a civil engineer for Los Angeles World Airports, said he was taken aback when Dr. Kit Miyamoto proposed the solution. "As an engineer, you are always taught that the more weight you put on a building, the worse it gets. When our consultants tell us we want to add 20 percent to the weight of the building and stick it on the top, we thought, 'Are you guys serious?'" said Markle.

Left: In February of 2007, a thousand-pound plaster panel fell off the Theme Building. Image courtesy of Gin Wong Associates and Miyamoto International. *Right:* The LAX Theme Building covered in scaffolding during arch repair. Image courtesy of Miyamoto International.

Image © Vince Tanzilli. Miyamoto International.

BUILT: 1960

AWARDED: 2010

ORIGINAL ARCHITECT:
Pereira & Luckman, Paul
Williams, Welton Becket

ARCHITECT: Gin Wong
Associates, Millard Lee, AIA

PROJECT MANAGER:
Los Angeles World Airports,
L. Scott Markle, SE

STRUCTURAL ENGINEER:
Miyamoto International, Inc.,
H. Kit Miyamoto, Ph.D.

STRUCTURAL ENGINEER: VCA
Engineers, Virgil Aoanan, PE

GENERAL CONTRACTOR:
Tower General Contractors,
Alex Guerrero

PALACE HOTEL SAN FRANCISCO

EVEN AFTER FORTY YEARS of working in the hotel, Palace Chief Engineer Jerry Turner steps into the Garden Court first thing each morning. "It's better than coffee—you step inside and you know it's a new day."

Illuminated by a translucent oblong dome with seventy thousand pieces of glass, the silvery four-story dining room transports visitors to the romantic San Francisco of a bygone era. Television personality Jan Yanehiro, who used to broadcast her *Evening Magazine* program from the room and still frequently dines there, said the Garden Court makes her feel grown up. "I'm a poor girl from Hawaii," she said. "Every time I walk in there I feel so sophisticated, so part of old-world San Francisco."

The original 1875 Palace Hotel was San Francisco's answer to casinos on the French Riviera. The visionary behind it was high-rolling financier William Chapman

Ralston, the "Magician of San Francisco." Facing financial ruin and the collapse of his Bank of California, Ralston didn't live long enough to see the hotel to completion. His body was found floating in the bay in August of 1875. Two months later the Palace opened, known popularly as the "Bonanza Inn."

From the beginning, the hotel's most distinctive space was the skylight-lit courtyard. For the first twenty-five years it was a carriage entrance, creating a grand first impression for visiting dignitaries like Ulysses S. Grant and William McKinley. During the great earthquake of 1906, the hotel held up quite well but was then engulfed in the fire that followed. When the hotel was rebuilt in 1908 in the Beaux-Arts style, the developers were inspired by the Grand Court to create the Garden Court, and once again the sunlight filtered down through the dome's iridescent glass. "Lovers of San Francisco, the Palace Hotel has risen again," said Mayor Edward Robeson Taylor on opening night. "We could scarcely think of San Francisco without the Palace Hotel."

Above left: Renovated hallway. *Above right and opposite:* Renovated Palace Restaurant. All images © Skidmore, Owings & Merrill LLP / © Heidrich Blessing.

By 1989 the Palace was looking a bit weary, and the owners decided it needed a full renovation. But just ten months into the job, the Bay Area was hit by the Loma Prieta quake. The temblor caused significant structural damage, and the renovation plans had to be redrawn to include a seismic retrofit. The glass dome's 692 geometric panels were taken down, cleaned, and replaced in a rebuilt armature under a new outer skylight. Ten chandeliers, each seven hundred pounds, were restored. A full seismic retrofit upgraded the building's steel frame and masonry-infill structural system with con-crete shear walls. Craftsmen carved molds to re-create the decorative plasterwork, and engineers performed light and shadow studies to ensure that the rebuilt dome would let in the same amount of illumination as the old one.

The hotel reopened on April 3, 1991, and the Garden Court has been busy ever since. "The Palace Hotel without the Garden Court would be just another hotel," said General Manager Clem Esmail. "There is no other room like it in the country, maybe the world."

Renovated entryway. Image © Skidmore, Owings & Merrill LLP/© Heidrich Blessing.

Renovated lobby and pool. Images © Skidmore, Owings & Merrill LLP /© Heidrich Blessing.

BUILT: 1909

AWARDED: 1989

ORIGINAL ARCHITECT:
Trowbridge & Livingston

PRESERVATION ARCHITECT:
Page & Turnbull

PROJECT ARCHITECT:
Skidmore, Owings & Merrill

GENERAL CONTRACTOR:
Swinerton Inc.

WOODLAND OPERA HOUSE WOODLAND

THEY CALLED IT Woodland Opera House, but really there was never much opera there. Rather, from its opening in 1885, the unassuming red-brick theater on downtown Woodland's Main Street hummed with no-frills entertainment for the hardworking agricultural community of the fertile valley.

Designed by Thomas J. Welsh, the masonry two-story, 450-seat theater is a classic nineteenth-century Ameri-

can playhouse: a proscenium arch with a horseshoe balcony, semicircular seating, and an orchestra pit. Handbills from the time advertise "Billy Pearl singing the latest Boston and New York craze 'Tommy, Tell Me True.'" On November 3, 1902, it was Anita Waldorf and Fiddle De De. *The Girl of the Golden West* came through town, starring Evelyn Vaughn. Boxing exhibitions slotted "Gentleman Jim" Corbett against John L. Sullivan. Dressing-room graffiti tells of "Musical comedians McCoy and Regan." Despite an 1892 fire that required much of the theater to be rebuilt, by 1913 more than three hundred touring companies had appeared on its stage.

But the music and the laughter abruptly stopped in 1913. Growing competition from the movie industry was already hurting the opera house's bottom line when one night a customer mistook a loading door for an exit. The patron broke his arm and sued, and the owners called it quits. It was a decision that would leave the building vacant for more than seventy years. Grass grew up around the moss-covered building. Kids broke in. A homeless man took up residence and set a back balcony bench ablaze trying to keep warm. Stories of the haunted opera house spread through Yolo County.

Somehow the obsolete theater survived, and California's fledgling preservation movement took notice. In 1971 the Yolo County Historical Society purchased the theater for $12,000. Five years later, California declared it a State Historic Park. After a $2 million restoration, it reopened in 1989, now structurally sound, with heat and air-conditioning, a sprinkler and alarm

Above left: Seating in theater, 1988. *Above right:* Chair seating, 1988. *Opposite:* Looking at the stage, 1988. All images courtesy of the California Preservation Foundation.

Image © 2005 Bev Sykes/Flickr/CC BY 2.0.

system, and access for disabled patrons. An annex was constructed for mechanical equipment, administrative office space, and a gift counter.

But it was really the granular detail of the restoration that preserved the theater's slightly shabby, creaky turn-of-the-century ambiance. Architect Ronald G. Brocchini tracked down original materials, fixtures, finishes, and colors. Gold-leaf wallpaper borders on the balcony ceilings were reproduced from fragments salvaged from crumbling walls. Persian Axminster carpets were imported from the original carpet mills in England. Aisle runners were made consistent with the original nineteenth-century installation: bound edges, the carpets tacked to the floor without padding. The-

ater seats were upholstered in traditional mohair, and electrified antique brass lighting fixtures matched the original gas-flame wall sconces and central chandelier.

Today the opera house, a National Register property, averages one hundred twenty stage performances a year, along with fifteen concerts, six dance recitals, four weddings, and fifty community meetings. Eight to twelve classes meet per week, and regular school performance days draw one thousand kids. The opera house is the only surviving theater in California that has never had a change of use. "If a person who lived in Yolo County one hundred years ago were to walk in here, it would be familiar to them; they would recognize it," said Theater Director Jeff Kean.

BUILT: 1885

AWARDED: 1989

ORIGINAL ARCHITECT:
Thomas J. Welsh

PROJECT ARCHITECT:
Gary Wirth

PRESERVATION ARCHITECT:
McCandless & Associates

INTERIOR DESIGNER:
Brocchini & Associates

MISSION INN RIVERSIDE

IN 1903 hotelier Frank Miller issued a promotional booklet for the inn he was expanding in Riverside.

In the pamphlet Miller called Riverside a "land of romance and mystery, where the gray walls of ancient missions awaken memories of mellow chimes." He didn't seem to mind that the town had never been home to any of California's twenty-one missions. "It is a pity that the old padres never saw the advantage of founding a mission in Riverside," he said. "But since they did not, we will bring the most beautiful features of each of the missions right here."

And so he did. Lifting design details from missions in Santa Barbara, Carmel, San Fernando, and San Juan Capistrano, Miller created what historian Kevin Starr has called a "Spanish Revival Oz: a neo-Franciscan fantasy of courts, patios, halls, archways, and domes."

For fifty-five years he never stopped building. Miller, who had bought the once modest roadhouse from his father at age twenty-three, built a two-hundred-room U-shaped structure with a "Courtyard of the Birds." Next came the Cloister Wing with its balconies, stained glass, and one-story flying buttresses arching

Above left: Archways in the Historic Rotunda, 1990. *Above right:* Door, 1990. *Previous page:* Mission Inn tower, 1990. All images courtesy of Architectural Resources Group.

over the sidewalk. On the roof is a replica of the red-domed Carmel Mission tower. Soon he was working on the Spanish Wing with its Author's Row built of red, hollow terra-cotta bricks. The last major addition was the International Rotunda, a six-story open cylindrical court crowned with a blue, gold, and white Amistad Dome.

Everywhere in the hotel are treasures that Miller brought back from his travels: a baptismal font from Taos, New Mexico, and a private altar from the mansion of the Marqués de Rayas in Guanajuato, Mexico. Miller built a shrine to aviators, and an elaborate wedding chapel with eight Tiffany art-glass windows. From the shrines of Europe and Asia came more than eight hundred bells, as well as crosses, fountains, and pagodas.

For decades the hotel attracted presidents and celebrities: Henry Ford, Amelia Earhart, W. C. Fields, Booker T. Washington, and Albert Einstein. The Nix-

Above left: Courtyard, 1990. *Above right:* Mission Inn tower and pool, view to the northeast. All images courtesy of Architectural Resources Group.

ons were married there. So was Bette Davis. Ronald and Nancy Reagan honeymooned there. Miller had an armchair built big enough to accommodate the girth of William Howard Taft, a gesture that was reportedly not appreciated by the 355-pound president.

After Frank Miller's death in 1935, the inn struggled. The days of wealthy easterners wintering in Southern California were waning. San Francisco hotel operator Ben Swig bought the hotel in 1956, and for the next twenty years the inn went through a series of sales, bankruptcies, repossessions, and ill-conceived renovations. By 1976 the situation was dire enough that the City of Riverside stepped in to buy it. After losing money on the hotel for eight years, the city sold it in 1985 for $3 million to the Carley Capital Group, which undertook a $30 million restoration.

The most egregious problems were in the hotel's oldest wing, the brick Mission Wing. Exterior walls

Image © Randall Michelson/rmpix.com.

were reinforced to meet seismic standards, sagging ceiling beams were shored up with steel plates, the original cast-iron columns were replaced with steel I-beams and anchored into reinforced concrete. The eastern wall of the Cloister Wing was strengthened, and the Spanish addition of the Rotunda Wing was reinforced as well. In 1992 Duane Roberts, a merchant banker who made a fortune selling frozen burritos, bought the hotel. He opened it a month later. "The Mission Inn is the fabric that binds the community together," Roberts told the *Orange County Resister.* "Some [wealthy] people have sports teams, I have my Mission Inn."

BUILT: 1902–1932

AWARDED: 1993

ENTRANT: Robert W. Klemme

ORIGINAL ARCHITECTS:
Arthur Benton, Myron Hunt, and G. Stanley Wilson

ARCHITECT:
WZMH Architects and ELS Architecture and Urban Design

PRESERVATION ARCHITECT:
Architectural Resources Group, Inc.

GENERAL CONTRACTOR:
Stolte Construction, Al Rensoner, Project Manager

TEMPLE OF KWAN TAI MENDOCINO

SOMETIMES BLOOD IS STRONGER than bricks and mortar. That is the case with Mendocino's Temple of Kwan Tai, a 264-square-foot bright green and red Taoist temple that for 160 years has sat perched on a foggy Mendocino hillside for one reason: a strong-willed family wanted it so.

The structure outlasted Mendocino's once bustling Chinatown. It stood guard as a mighty logging industry rose and fell, as Skunk Train steam locomotives disappeared from the redwood forests between Gualala and Westport, as steam lumber schooners vanished from the coast. Built for just $14 in materials, the modest temple is a testament to the strength of a family vow.

"There was a promise passed down from generation to generation to preserve and protect the temple," said Lorraine Hee-Chorley, whose great-grandfather founded the Kwan Tai. "Before we could walk, my father was asking us to make that same promise."

In 1854 a Chinese junk landed in the town of Caspar, just north of Mendocino. One of the passengers on the boat was Lee Sing John, the great-grandfather of Hee-Chorley. While there is some disagreement about the exact year the temple was erected, there is evidence that Lee Sing John and other immigrants had completed it by 1854. During that time, the Chinese were settling into Mendocino, drawn to coastal communities rich in lumber, seaweed, and albacore. The newcomers cooked in the camps, opened sundry shops, and worked as "water slingers," responsible for keeping the trails wet so cut logs slid more easily. At its height in the 1860s and 1870s, the Chinese population in Mendocino topped six hundred.

The temple has two doors, three windows, and a gable roof. It is dedicated to Kwan Tai—a Taoist symbol of integrity and loyalty. Above the door are written the Chinese characters spelling *Mo Dai Miu,* which means "Military God-King Temple." In the main altar is an image bordered in seashell of Kwan Tai flanked by generals Liu Bei and Zhang Fei. The temple has nine steps, a lucky number in Chinese architecture because it is said to fend off evil spirits.

Even after Mendocino's Chinatown burned down in 1910 and anti-Chinese laws made the territory less than hospitable, the descendants of Lee Sing John stuck around. Yip Lee, daughter of the temple's founder, had ten children, one of whom was George Hee, father of daughters Lorraine Hee-Chorley and Loretta Hee McCoard. Growing up, Hee-Chorley and her six brothers and sisters were the only Chinese in Mendocino. Their house wrapped around the temple, which stood out as the most brightly painted structure in the subdued city. "It was the only piece of history that told us that the Chinese were in Mendocino County," said Hee-Chorley.

In 1995 the family deeded the property to a nonprofit organization devoted to Chinese immigrant history on

Above left: Image © Deena Zarlin. *Above right:* Image © Wendy Roberts. *Opposite:* Restored altar. Image © Tony Eppstein. *Previous page:* Image © Tony Eppstein.

the north coast. In 1998 the temple underwent a renovation that included a new foundation and a new shake redwood roof and siding. The most shocking construction defect was discovered on the east side of the temple. Upon pulling the skirting away, the restoration team found the posts dangling in the air rather than sunk into the proper concrete footings. "Some people said it was a miracle that the building didn't blow over, but I would say it was Kwan Tai and the gods inside who made sure it was still standing," said Hee-Chorley.

BUILT: 1854

AWARDED: 2002

OWNER: Temple of Kwan Tai, Inc.

ORIGINAL ARCHITECT: N/A

PRINCIPAL ARCHITECT,
HISTORIC PRESERVATION
CONSULTANT: Carey & Co. Inc.,
Alice Carey

LEAD ENGINEER:
I. L. Welty and Associates

GENERAL CONTRACTOR:
Pollard Construction, Don Pollard

LOCKE BOARDING HOUSE LOCKE

ON A PER-CAPITA BASIS, Locke must be the most studied and well-documented town in California. The century-old rural Chinatown on the delta has been exhaustively chronicled, filmed, and debated. There are dissertations, historical fictions, and documentary films. The book *Bitter Melon* (Heyday, 1987) captures the stories of nearly every surviving citizen. The California State Legislature, the California Department of Parks and Recreation, and the Sacramento Housing and Redevelopment Agency have all held hearings on the fate of the little town.

Yet for all the attention, policy makers and preservationists have struggled to figure out how to make Locke a real twenty-first-century town without sacrificing its charm and historical architectural integrity—the ramshackle dilapidation that makes it so appealing. "How do you maintain the essential qualities of a historic place when one of its endearing qualities is deterioration?" said Stephen Farneth of Architectural Resources Group, an architecture firm specializing in preservation. That was the challenge facing the preservation team as it set about restoring the boarding house, which was built to provide shelter for the semi-migrant Chinese agricultural workers who populated the town in its prime but were not allowed to own land there under the 1882 Chinese Exclusion Act.

Built with Chinese capital and Chinese labor, Locke was developed mostly in 1914 and 1915. By 1909 the Southern

Images this page, opposite page, and next page courtesy of Architectural Resources Group.

Pacific Railroad had constructed a line from Sacramento to Walnut Grove to facilitate the exportation of asparagus and celery. The railroad company built a packing shed along the Sacramento River, just north of Walnut Grove. On land owned by the Locke family, entrepreneur Chan Tin San added a one-story store and saloon for the workers. When a fire wiped out Walnut Grove's Chinatown, many Chinese heeded Chan Tin San's call to relocate to Locke instead of rebuilding in Walnut Grove. The rapid growth of Locke had a lot to do with the persuasive personality of Chan Tin San, according to Ping Lee in *Bitter Melon*. "He was a big man, a real fireball."

Before long, Locke had six hundred residents, nine markets, four restaurants, two slaughterhouses, five gambling houses, a flour mill, and five brothels. Boarding houses lined the main street. Workers from surrounding communities flocked to Locke to blow off steam after long weeks of packing asparagus or prunes. But the town started losing population after World War II. By 1970 there were 150 Chinese residents. By 1980 the Chinese population had shrunk to forty-two. By 2012 Locke was home to sixty-two residents,

including eleven Chinese Americans. Today the barely inhabited rustic town is a National Historic Landmark District that feels a bit like an old Chinese ghost town, one windstorm away from collapse.

The restored 1921 boarding house, constructed by Japanese immigrants Sukeichi and Nobu Kuramoto, offers a blueprint for how some of the other structures might be shored up against further decay. The building, which the Kuramotos had rented to seasonal workers for $2.50 a month, was shabbily built and on the verge of collapsing when the preservationists started working on it. The challenge was how to stabilize it while "retaining the original materials and, most importantly, retaining the shack quality of its construction," explained Farneth. The restoration team put in a foundation and replaced some of the deteriorated wood siding. Windows were restored, even though they were in bad shape. Makeshift repairs like sheet-metal patches placed over knotholes were kept in place. "Those things helped define the low-level vernacular quality of the building," said Farneth. "The character was what we were trying to preserve."

BUILT: 1921

AWARDED: 2011

ORIGINAL ARCHITECT: N/A

PROJECT MANAGER:
Sacramento Housing and Redevelopment Agency, Kevin Odell

PRINCIPAL-IN-CHARGE:
Architectural Resources Group, Inc., Stephen Farneth, FAIA

PRINCIPAL CONSERVATOR:
Architectural Resources Group, Inc., David Wessel, Mary Slater

STRUCTURAL ENGINEER:
SOHA Engineers, Art Dell

CIVIL ENGINEER:
R.E.Y. Engineers, David Sagan

GENERAL CONTRACTOR:
Reyman Brothers Construction, Kenneth Reyman

ANTELOPE VALLEY INDIAN MUSEUM LANCASTER

HOWARD ARDEN EDWARDS was a novelist, high school teacher, painter, naturalist, poet, theatrical set designer, carpenter, and amateur archeologist. A farmer he was not.

That did not prevent him, however, from filing a homesteading application in 1928 staking a claim to 160 acres in Antelope Valley, on the western tip of the

Mojave Desert, situated between the Tehachapi and San Gabriel Mountains. In adherence to the National Homestead Act of 1862, intended by the United States government to convert federal land into small family farms, Edwards planted twenty acres of barley at the cost of $124. The barley quickly died. Edwards, who painted sets in Hollywood and taught design classes at Lincoln High School in Los Angeles, had somehow neglected to provide water for his desert crop. (He didn't get around to installing a well until 1932.)

But what he lacked in agricultural common sense he made up for on the rest of the property. He handcrafted a forty-by-sixty-foot ad hoc Bavarian chalet that incorporated the steep rock formation beneath. The railings and furniture were made of Joshua tree branches; walls and steps were carved out of the sloped quartz monzonite on the hillside. The stairs between the two rooms passed through a narrow crevice in the rock outcrop. The fieldstone chimney in the living room was also built into a natural rock crevice.

Edwards, a former traveling-circus clown, was adept at finding ways to augment his modest teacher's salary. Inside his chalet he created a world inspired by the Native American cultures he had studied in the Southwest and California. On sheets salvaged from movie and theater sets, he painted bright images inspired by the kachina figures of the Pueblo people. On the walls

Above left: Stainless steel wires, differentiated from the historic fabric of the building and designed to be unobtrusive and reversible, were strategically placed to increase stability. *Above right:* Kachina Hall looking south. *Opposite:* The new roofing system was built around the decorative murals. All images © Stephen Schafer.

Top: The museum is set into the south slopes of Piute Butte near Lancaster. *Bottom:* North wall of Kachina Hall and view into the Southwest Room (stairs on the left lead to California Hall). All images © Stephen Schafer.

he displayed pottery, tools, and other artifacts found on his travels. He called the building Yato Kya, "Rancho of the Sun," as well as the Antelope Valley Indian Research Museum. He charged visitors admission and produced elaborate theatrical productions under the moonlight that were significant enough to draw critics from the *Los Angeles Times* into the desert to review them.

Edwards eventually grew tired of Yato Kya. He sold the property to Grace Wilcox Oliver, a Hollywood entrepreneur with a degree in anthropology, who expanded the museum's collection. The property later briefly became a dude ranch, before Oliver's daughter began a campaign to preserve the deteriorating structures and collections. The State of California took over the museum in the 1980s and it was revived as the Antelope Valley Indian Museum State Park.

Today visitors to Yato Kya no longer can enjoy Edward's pageants. But much of the house is just as Edwards left it—except better protected against earthquakes and the Mojave climate. For years the desert's extreme climate fluctuations—temperatures reach 110 in the summer and drop below freezing on winter nights—took their toll on the house and artifacts. The museum was cooled with swamp coolers, which created humid tropical conditions inside the build-

ing. Objects cracked and grew moldy as the air gained and lost humidity. The building swayed and creaked as wind gusted across the desert. Rain seeped in where the museum's roofs joined together.

In 2009 the museum was in need of structural strengthening, a climate-control system, and insulation. A stabilization project included installation of a geothermal exchange climate-control system for the museum—deep wells that take advantage of the stable temperature and humidity found deep underground. The building was especially flimsy and it was a challenge to strengthen it, said preservation architect John D. Lasek, a partner with Page & Turnbull. Sixteen "collar tie" cables bolted the outside of the building to the rock formations beneath. Three and a half inches of insulation were added to the roof.

While his flowery notions of Native American life were not historically accurate, Edwards was more progressive than most collectors of Native artifacts in that era. "A lot of the private collectors were looking for beautiful pots. He was out there collecting scraps of rope and food," said Museum Curator Peggy Ronning. "He was a little ahead of his time in being interested in the entirety of what people's lives were like. He was not some Indiana Jones in search of treasure."

BUILT: 1928

AWARDED: 2011

OWNER: California State Parks, Kathy Weatherman

ORIGINAL DESIGNER: Howard Arden Edwards

ARCHITECT: Page & Turnbull, John D. Lesak, AIA, FAPT, LEED AP

EXECUTIVE ARCHITECT AND STRUCTURAL ENGINEER: Wiss, Janney, Elstner Associates, Inc., Gary Searer

GENERAL CONTRACTOR: Bowe Contractors, Darin Bowe

EL CAPITAN OFFICE AND THEATRE LOS ANGELES

IN JUNE OF 1991, after a $14 million restoration, Hollywood's El Capitan Theatre reopened with the period superhero adventure film *The Rocketeer.* As the lights dimmed and theatergoers settled into plush new seats, a sparkly silver curtain drew open, illuminated by floodlights, border lamps, and balcony spotlights. Behind that curtain was not the screen but another gold curtain, which opened to reveal...another curtain. The fourth and final curtain was a black velour drape with a painted scene of the Hollywood skyline and a silhouette of Fred Astaire dancing with Ginger Rogers. It was classic El Capitan showmanship harkening back to the days when a "four-curtain" theater represented the pinnacle of movie-palace pedigree.

Along with the Egyptian Theatre and the Chinese Theatres, the El Capitan was one of a trio of over-the-top venues developed by Charles "The Father of Hollywood" Toberman. El Capitan debuted on May 3, 1926, with the play *Charlot's Revue*. The next day, the Sunday *Los Angeles Times* front-page headline stated "Dazzling Opening for Hollywood's First Home of Spoken Drama." With its cast-concrete Spanish Colonial exterior and $1.2 million East Indian interior design created by San Francisco architect G. Albert Lansburgh, the venue also advertised the "most beautiful usherettes" in L.A.

Between 1926 and 1936, 120 plays were produced at the El Capitan, including *No, No, Nanette* and *Anything Goes*. Will Rogers and Clark Gable strutted the stage.

Above left: From Hollywood Boulevard, 1997. *Above right*: Theater lobby detail, 1997. *Opposite*: Hollywood Boulevard Office Tower entry hallway, 1997. All images © Marvin Rand Estate.

During the Depression, as revenues for live theater dropped off, the El Capitan made the transition to film. In 1941 *Citizen Kane* made its world premiere there, after which the theater closed for remodeling. A year later, it was reborn as the Hollywood Paramount, a sleek, new "Art Moderne" movie house.

The theater was the West Coast flagship for Paramount until 1948, when the US Supreme Court ruled that movie studios had to divest themselves of their distribution and theater holdings. Operators came and went until the late 1980s, when movie companies were allowed to own theaters again. The Walt Disney Company entered into a lease to take over the venue.

Disney spared no expense to rehabilitate the interior spaces. Layers of mustard-yellow paint were stripped away, and the opera boxes, which had been removed in 1941, were re-created. The original lobby, long since demolished, was reproduced from photographs. The team made molds of existing parts of the proscenium, and then re-created it. In came a giant 1929 Wurlitzer theater organ originally built for San Francisco's Fox Theatre. Disney commissioned the West Coast Trimming Corporation to make eight tassels for the proscenium. Each tassel was three and a half feet long. "There hasn't been a theater in sixty years with tassels this big," said the late theater designer Joseph Musil, who worked on the project.

After the 1991 opening, architecture critic Aaron Betsky called the refurbished theater an "illusion of a spectacle" steeped in a "peasant baroque" Churrigueresque style "updated with Art Deco dash." He wrote in the *Los Angeles Times*, "Every square inch of El Capitan is painted, gilded or stenciled. The interior is a tapestry in three dimensions, a coat of so many colors that the eye is dazzled into the kind of suspension of belief demanded both in a theater and for the appreciation of this kind of eclectic architecture."

Today the El Capitan is an exclusive first-run theater for Walt Disney and features live performances before every show. Disney also bought the Masonic Temple building next door; on Oscars night the two classic structures provide a vintage backdrop for red-carpet festivities. Los Angeles Conservancy Executive Director Linda Dishman said the restoration of the El Capitan came at a time when many of Hollywood's older buildings needed love. "Just as important was that it was Disney that took the lead," she said. "It was a strong statement from a major entertainment company that they saw value in preserving this theater and it being a focal point in Hollywood."

BUILT: 1926

AWARDED: 1991 AND 1999

OWNER: CIMCO

ORIGINAL ARCHITECT:
G. Albert Lansburgh

ARCHITECT: John Ash Group,
John Ash

STRUCTURAL ENGINEER:
Ismail Associates, Inc.

GENERAL CONTRACTOR:
RJT Construction

GENERAL CONTRACTOR:
S & T Development

MALIBU PIER MALIBU

THE CREAKY WOODEN Malibu Pier, with its diving pelicans and adjacent three-point break, holds a mythic place in the American imagination.

In the summer of 1956 teenager Kathy Kohner drove the family car to Malibu Lagoon from Brentwood and caught her first wave. The mostly teenage boy surfers took to her and nicknamed her Gidgit. Her father,

screenwriter Frederick Kohner, wrote a book about the summer. The book became a bestseller, Gidgit a pop sensation. Malibu became a billion-dollar brand that companies like Quicksilver used to sell swimming trunks and surfboards.

These days Quicksilver products are as close as most people get to the real Malibu. Next to the Malibu

Lagoon is a fence separating the narrow public beach from the houses on stilts that are home to the likes of Brad Pitt, Leonardo DiCaprio, and Jennifer Aniston. "In Malibu it's hard to get the locals to come out— people move to Malibu to hide," said California State Parks Supervising Historian James D. Newland.

But in 2005, San Francisco attorney and real-estate investor Alexander Leff had a vision for reviving Malibu's most famous icon. Leff, who has had a place in Malibu over the years, was reading the local newspaper when he saw that State Parks was looking for a concessionaire to take over the pier, which had been closed for a decade. Leff responded to the request for proposals and was selected to take it over. "The pier is the epitome of that romantic view of the good life of Southern California," said Leff. "After driving [Interstate 10] through the smog and through the malls, you come to Malibu Pier and say, 'Ah ha. This is what it was all about, and is all about.'"

Malibu Pier was built in 1905 to support the business operations of Frederick Hastings Rindge. Hides, grains, fruits, and vegetables were shipped from the pier while construction supplies and other provisions came in. The Rindge family was intensely private and hired guards to evict all trespassers. They successfully fought the intrusion of public roads and railroads onto the pristine waterfront until 1929, when the Pacific Coast Highway was built.

Opened to the public in 1934, the pier was home to a fleet of sports-fishing boats until World War II, when it served as a US Coast Guard daylight lookout station. But it fell on hard times, in part due to storm damage, and was closed to the public in 1995.

In 2008 Malibu Pier reopened after a restoration that was a joint effort between Leff's group and State Parks, which owns it. The pier superstructure was rehabilitated, its four 1940s-era buildings restored. About 60 percent of the original wooden siding was preserved. Workers removed the slab floor that had been poured over the original wooden floor. The buildings were revived with a nostalgic yacht-club vibe: glossy white wood interior, stuffed marlins, sea-green booths.

"The goal was to keep it to the historic period of the pier, the feel of 1945 to 1960," Newland said.

Since the restoration, business has been challenging. The first restaurant operator Leff brought in went out of business in 2012, and Leff decided to take over the operation himself. He is optimistic he will be able to capture Malibu's "dress-down glamour of blue jeans and flip-flops."

"What is a wooden pier? It's a place where kids play and fish, young people hold hands and kiss, and lonely old men like me gaze off into the distance and meditate," said Leff. "We all know what that is about. So the job of doing the interiors is to be consistent with what people thought about Malibu and be consistent with a wooden pier, which has something that's a little gritty, a little funky, a little rough-hewn."

BUILT: 1905

AWARDED: 2009

ORIGINAL ARCHITECT: Unknown

STATE HISTORIAN/ PRESERVATION SPECIALIST: California State Parks, Southern Service Center, James D. Newland

BUILDING RESTORATION ARCHITECT: California State Parks, Southern Service Center, Carl Schaffer

ARCHITECT/PRESERVATION CONSULTANT: Historic Resources Group, Peyton Hall, FAIA

STRUCTURAL ENGINEER: CYS Structural Engineers, Inc., Kenneth Luttrell

BUILDING RESTORATION CONTRACTOR: Dennis J. Amoroso Construction, Jim Bennison

PIER STABILIZATION CONTRACTOR: Meek Construction Company, Jim Jilk

PLACES OF CONGREGATION

Some public buildings are exquisitely planned civic treasures that represent the finest design and construction a broad community has to offer. Others have narrower purpose: a home amid a diverse city, carved out by an ethnic or religious group. Still others are places built to meet a perceived economic, transportation, or political need.

Temple Sherith Israel. Image © David Wakely.

LOS ANGELES PUBLIC LIBRARY, CENTRAL BRANCH
LOS ANGELES

THE DEMOLITION OF THE original Penn Station coalesced a previously unorganized preservation movement in New York. In Boston it was the obliteration of the old West End neighborhood to make way for high-rises, hospitals, and a new government center. In Los Angeles, it was the threat to the Central Library. But luckily, the outcry came before the wrecking ball.

The final work of architect Bertram Goodhue, the Los Angeles Central Library opened in 1926. The third

Above: The rotunda's restored murals, decorative stenciling, and zodiac chandelier, 1993. *Previous page:* Children's reading room, 1993. Both images ©
Foaad Farah.

Left: Reading area in the Tom Bradley Wing stacks, 1993. *Right*: Restored light fixtures and stenciling, 1993. Both images © Foaad Farah.

largest library in the United States (after those in New York and Chicago), its skyscraper-like profile speaks to early modernism while much of the building's details draw from a roster of ancient cultures. A city proclamation issued for the 1926 dedication summarized: "It follows no accented order of architecture, but through it strains of the Spanish, of the East, of the modern European, come and go like folk songs in a great symphony, rising to new and undreamed-of heights in an order truly American in spirit."

Cosmic wonders meet California history and odes to learning throughout the building. The central tower is topped with a tiled mosaic featuring a hand holding a torch that represents the "Light of Learning." The second floor is a high-domed rotunda exploding with light and color: at its center, an illuminated blue-and-green glass globe chandelier is decorated with the signs of the zodiac. On the surrounding walls, twelve murals painted by Dean Cornwell in 1933 show scenes from the history of California.

By the 1960s, as downtown Los Angeles grew into a high-rise office district, pressure grew to free up the library land for development. At the same time, the library was beginning to show its age. In a 1966 editorial the *Los Angeles Times* deplored the condition of the building, calling it "woefully inadequate."

"There is no air-conditioning, few fans, and poor ventilation, forcing librarians and users to endure suffocatingly hot summers and cold, drafty winters," the editorial stated. "No provisions are made for the proper care and shelving of rare books: in one case, a Fourth Folio edition of Shakespeare is kept in a lavatory wrapped in blankets."

A proposal to move the Central Library to the Westside of L.A. in the mid-1970s prompted a loose group of opponents to the redevelopment to form the Los Angeles Conservancy to fight it. In 1983, after several years of debate, the city council directed the Community Redevelopment Agency to preserve the library. The firm of Hardy Holzman Pfeiffer Associates was picked to restore the original building and design a large addition to the library's east side. The city paid for the projects partly by selling air rights above the library to a private developer across the street, a move that resulted in a one-thousand-foot Library Tower (now the US Bank Tower).

But what was accomplished through grassroots politics was almost undone by arsonists. Two fires in 1986, before the renovation had started, destroyed portions of the library's collections and damaged many of the interior decorations. The first fire charred four hundred thousand volumes worth $22 million. Conservators from the Getty Museum rushed to the scene

Left: Exterior wall detail of the Tom Bradley Wing addition, 1993. *Right:* South facade after renovation, 1993. Both images © Foaad Farah.

to help save fire- and water-damaged books, stencils, murals, and other artwork.

The library was reopened in April 1993. Today the 550,000-square-foot facility functions as a research center and headquarters for 66 branches. In addition to 90 linear miles of shelving and seating for 1,500 patrons, the library features a conference center, a 235-seat multimedia auditorium, a cafe, a bookstore, and 1.3 acres of public space. A marble bench sits on the landing between the first and second floors. Inscribed on it are the words *Dei Gratia,* Latin for "Thank God." As in "Thank God this place wasn't destroyed."

BUILT: 1926

AWARDED: 1994

OWNER:
Los Angeles Public Library

ORIGINAL ARCHITECT:
Bertram Goodhue

ARCHITECT: Hardy Holzman Pfeiffer Associates

ENGINEER: Hayakawa Associates

CONSULTANT: Tatyana M. Thompson and Associates, Inc.

GENERAL CONTRACTOR:
Tutor Saliba Corporation

Detail of restored stenciled ceiling, 1993. Image © Foaad Farah.

GRIFFITH OBSERVATORY LOS ANGELES

AS THE DATE of a May 2012 solar eclipse approached, workers at the Griffith Observatory scurried around getting ready. They set up extra telescopes and binoculars with special filters to allow the public to view the eclipse. They stocked the observatory gift shop with 2,500 pairs of special eclipse glasses. It turned out 2,500 wasn't nearly enough. Forty-eight hours before the eclipse, the glasses were sold out, $2.99 a pair.

It seems that in Los Angeles, a city full of stars, the cosmos has a large following. As one of the world's first public centers for astronomy and science education, the Griffith Observatory has long been one of California's most cherished institutions. Situated on expansive grounds with a sweeping view of the L.A. Basin, the building's Art Deco design, its Greek and Beaux-Arts architectural details, and its murals, sculptures, and installations fill two million visitors a year with a sense of cosmic wonder. Longtime director Edwin Krupp

calls the triple-domed Griffith Observatory "the hood ornament of Los Angeles."

In 1896 Welsh-born mining mogul Griffith J. Griffith donated three thousand acres of Rancho Los Feliz to the City of Los Angeles to create a "great park" as "a place of rest and relaxation for the masses." Years later, peering through the telescope at the nearby Mount Wilson Observatory, he had a revelation: "If all

Above left: Workers installing new copper on the planetarium dome, 2004. Image courtesy of Levin & Associates. *Above right:* The observation terrace after restoration, 2006. Image © Tim Griffith. *Opposite:* Image © 2006 Tim Griffith.

Top: The Café at the End of the Universe, which was built into the western slope of the hill, 2006. *Bottom:* The West Alcoves exhibit hall, 2006. Both images © Tim Griffith.

mankind could look through that telescope, it would change the world."

Opened in 1935 at the end of the Great Depression, the Griffith Observatory quickly became one of the most visited landmarks in Southern California. It was built during an era when goods and labor were cheap, and the building exterior reflects a wide range of detail, including the Greek key pattern cast directly into the concrete; the bronze and glass on the main entrance doors; the decorative metal window grilles; the copper-covered domes; and the Astronomers Monument, a WPA-funded concrete sculpture on the front lawn.

The interior of the observatory was designed with the most expensive materials of the day, including travertine, marble, ornate wood and bronze metalwork. The design of the public spaces, particularly the alcoves, was intended to convey a sense of monumentality and importance consistent with the cosmic topics presented.

By 2002, however, many of the observatory's once innovative features were outdated, and sixty-seven years of continuous use had resulted in wear, both inside and out. The challenges were significant. The telescope domes, cupola, terraces, walls, murals, flooring, artwork, and exterior landscaping were cleaned, repaired, and updated. Expansion came in the form of a forty-thousand-square-foot addition under the observatory's front lawn. The approach taken by the architecture team of Pfeiffer Partners and Levin & Associates created a new space that "met the needs of the institution in a way that didn't detract from the historical building," said Linda Dishman, director of the Los Angeles Conservancy.

After the $93 million renovation, which included $25.6 million in private funds, the Griffith Observatory reopened in 2006. It was obvious that a city landmark had been preserved, enlarged, and enhanced. And with it, something more important had been preserved: the opportunity for everyone to leave Los Angeles for the day and explore the vast cosmos. "This place isn't about astronomy—it's about astronomy and people," said Krupp. And the Hollywood take on the universe beyond is underscored by the bronze bust outside the domed building: James Dean—a reminder that the observatory plays a starring role in *Rebel Without a Cause*.

BUILT: 1935	ORIGINAL ARCHITECT: John C. Austin and Frederick M. Ashley	STRUCTURAL ENGINEER: Miyamoto International, Inc.
AWARDED: 2007		
OWNER: City of Los Angeles Department of Parks and Recreation	EXECUTIVE AND DESIGN ARCHITECT: Pfeiffer Partners	GENERAL CONTRACTOR: S. J. Amoroso Construction
	PRESERVATION AND ASSOCIATE ARCHITECT: Levin & Associates Architects	

STANFORD MEMORIAL CHURCH PALO ALTO

WHEN STANFORD MEMORIAL CHURCH reopened in 1993 after a three-year closure for post–Loma Prieta earthquake repairs, couples lined up to see wedding coordinator Betsy Koester. Some of them had been waiting a long time.

"I had one moving letter from a man who had postponed his wedding plans in order to be married in the church," Koester told the *Stanford News Service*. Every year about two hundred weddings are held at the church, with a back-to-back five-wedding marathon every Saturday. But for generations the church, which the Stanford community refers to as MemChu, has represented more than a place to exchange vows. It has been the focal point of the university's historic main quad, the spiritual center of the campus, and a place that has been on the forefront of social and political change, from Vietnam War protests to the more recent push for the legalization of same-sex marriage.

Stanford benefactor Jane Stanford built the church as a memorial to her husband, railroad magnate and governor Leland Stanford, who passed away in 1893, two years after the university opened and six years before construction started on the church. The Stanfords had named the university after their only child, Leland Jr., who died of typhoid fever in 1884 at age fifteen. "While my whole heart is in the university, my soul is in that church," said Jane Stanford.

Designed by architect Charles A. Coolidge, Stanford Memorial Church was inspired by the Piazza San Marco in Venice and other European cathedrals that Stanford had visited. With carved natural buff sandstone, large columns, low archways, and terra-cotta roofs, the church takes freely from the palettes of a variety of architecture styles, including Romanesque, California Mission, Art Nouveau, Pre-Raphaelite, and Byzantine.

Above left: Crossing arches with the northeast pendente angel. *Above right:* Detail of door and gold tesserae mosaic walls in the balcony of the east transept. Both images © Russell Abraham, Pfeiffer Partners. *Opposite:* Stanford Memorial Church at dusk. Image © Jill Clardy.

Above: The restored central dome, skylight, and plasterwork, with the mosaic pendente angels. *Opposite:* Balcony in the west transept. Both images © Russell Abraham, Pfeiffer Partners.

The sandstone arches, borders, and pillar capitals took more than two years to carve, and Jane Stanford carried a parasol that was notched at the end to measure the increasing depth of the carvings. The church's buff-colored exterior contrasts with its dimly lit interior, a glistening procession of carved stone, polished wood, stained glass, and Venetian glass mosaics. Jane Stanford, who was said to have had a "Victorian aversion to blank space," pushed for both interior and exterior mosaics, which took workmen two years to complete, using tiles in twenty thousand shades of color as well as real gold leaf.

Much of the church was damaged and rebuilt after the 1906 earthquake. The church was shaken up again in the 1989 quake, when the four mosaic angels in the pendentives supporting the dome crumbled and an eight-foot mosaic section of an angel's wing crashed seventy feet to the floor. A year later, Pfeiffer Partners oversaw the development of a structural evaluation report and its subsequent implementation, including the restoration of architectural components. An effort to invisibly strengthen the center portion of the church led to behind-the-scenes steel and concrete reinforcement, and the opportunity for an overall renovation.

While most universities are organized around libraries, Jane Stanford felt that "the education which the students are receiving is secondary, if a religious and spiritual influence is not exerted over them." Stanford also insisted that the church be ecumenical and that the murals and mosaics portray women prominently. When Stanford's Memorial Church was dedicated in the winter of 1903, ministers from thirteen Christian denominations were in attendance, as was a rabbi.

Stanford's beliefs are carved into the church's east transept. "Religion is intended as a comfort, a solace, a necessity to the soul's welfare," the inscription reads. "Whichever form of religion offers the greatest comfort, the greatest solace, it is the form which should be adopted."

BUILT: 1903

AWARDED: 1993

ORIGINAL ARCHITECT:
Charles A. Coolidge

OWNER: Stanford University, with Stanford University Architect and Stanford University Facilities Management, Project Managers

STRUCTURAL ENGINEER:
Degenkolb Engineers

CONSERVATOR: DeYoung Museum, Lesley Bone

ARCHITECT: Pfeiffer Partners

GENERAL CONTRACTOR:
Dinwiddie Construction Company

Detail of the southwest pendente angel, one of the four mosaic pendente angels between the crossing arches, which were part of the original structure. Image © Russell Abraham, Pfeiffer Partners.

SAN FRANCISCO CITY HALL SAN FRANCISCO

ARCHITECTS JEFFREY HELLER and Clark Manus were a few years into preconstruction work for the seismic retrofit and modernization of San Francisco City Hall when Willie Brown was elected mayor in 1995. It didn't take long for them to figure out that the renovation would not be business as usual. "I got a call from [then City Architect] Tony Irons. He sits me down and says Willie is the mayor now and he wants the building to be a great building," recalled Heller.

And $293 million later—$100 million over the original budget—Heller and Manus understood.

Completed in 1915, San Francisco City Hall has never lacked for self-regard. Designed by Bakewell and Brown, the building's 307-foot dome is the tallest

Above left: Applying gold leaf to the dome. *Above right*: The dome at evening. *Opposite*: Restored Council Chamber. *Previous page*: Exterior after renovation. All images © Robert Canfield Photography.

Left: Interior rotunda and stairway after renovation. *Right:* Rotunda ceiling. Both images © Robert Canfield Photography.

in the United States, 42 feet higher than the capital dome in Washington, DC. The rotunda is decked out with Tennessee pink marble floors, Colorado limestone walls, and four medallions created by the sculptor Henri Crenier representing equality, liberty, strength, and learning. On the east wall is Father Time, an hourglass in his hand. Under him an inscription reads: "San Francisco, oh glorious City of our hearts that has been tried and found not wanting. Go thou with like spirit to make the future thine." The wood paneling in the Board of Supervisors Chamber is Manchurian oak, while the benches, railings, and desks in the chamber are a harder California oak. The plasterwork above the public speaking area has four demon heads. (Rumor has it that this was done because the public always made trouble for the elected officials.)

In 1964 Joseph A. Baird Jr., curator and art consultant to the California Historical Society, wrote that city hall "is basically a rather pompous building on the outside." On the inside, however, he said it is "worthy of comparison with the best of the late Baroque, and superior in design to the Paris Opera with which it might be generally evaluated."

By the time Brown took office, the building's grandeur had faded, its walls cracked by the 1989 Loma Prieta earthquake. The twin north and south light courts were essentially dark courts, covered up with nine-foot drop ceilings and clogged with cubicles. City workers were crammed into every available nook in the building, including back hallways, closets, and mezzanines. Upon taking office Mayor Brown found the building a "dull, stultifying place, grimy and gloomy....It was just being rehabbed, not restored the way it should have been," he wrote in his memoir, *Basic Brown*.

At the time, San Francisco voters had already approved bond money to protect the building against future earthquakes with a base-isolation system: six hundred great rubber-and-steel disks installed under each column to permit the building to absorb shocks. But it was the building's more visible and glamorous aspects that Mayor Brown wanted to shine. He fought to restore the building's light courts as ceremonial rooms open to the public, rather than the hodge-podge of office spaces they had become. This meant relocating about three hundred city workers, whom Brown at one point, in perhaps a poor choice of words, described as "pencil pushers."

Brown's crowning desire was to put gold leaf on the dome. But finding $500,000 for the 23.5-carat gold leafing required some creative thinking, which eventually came from Heller. San Francisco required that developers set aside 1 percent of a project budget for public art. Why couldn't the dome be considered public art? Legislation was hastily written to broaden the law so it would apply to the city hall dome.

When the building opened, Gladys Hansen, the city's archivist emeritus, told the *New York Times* that San Francisco was in need of this new symbol. "We've lived too long on the reputation of our bridges," she said

BUILT: 1915

AWARDED: 2000

OWNER: City and County of San Francisco

ORIGINAL ARCHITECT: Bakewell and Brown

PROJECT LEAD ARCHITECT: City of San Francisco, Tony Irons, City Architect

CONSULTING ARCHITECT: Heller Manus Architects

ARCHITECT: San Francisco Bureau of Architecture

PRESERVATION ARCHITECT AND CONSULTANT: Carey & Co. Inc.

LEAD ENGINEER: Forell/Elsesser Engineers, Inc.

GENERAL CONTRACTOR: Huber Hunt & Nichols

PASADENA CITY HALL PASADENA

THE CITY HALLS IN Pasadena and San Francisco are kindred buildings. They share an architectural firm—San Francisco–based Bakewell and Brown. Both buildings are West Coast examples of the Beaux-Arts City Beautiful Movement. Both are magnets for brides and grooms with their roses, diamond rings, and flash-bulb entourages.

Despite these similarities, the two landmarks are as different as Southern California is from the Bay Area. If San Francisco City Hall exudes formality and worldly sophistication, Pasadena City Hall is its more open, extroverted Southern Californian cousin. Instead of wood-paneled double-loaded corridors, the walkways from one department to another snake through a Spanish Colonial courtyard with a Baroque cast-stone fountain, rose bushes, and oak and magnolia trees. If sunlight is the best disinfectant, the bright Pasadena City Hall seems to embody a clean and transparent home for governing.

The building benefited from having San Francisco designers, said project preservation architect Stephen Farneth of Architectural Resources Group. "It was Northern California architects who may have been much more open to the opportunities of climate than if it had been Southern California architects," he said.

Planned in 1922 during the City Beautiful Movement, Pasadena City Hall was the centerpiece of a city that George Bernard Shaw dubbed the "Athens of the West." Rising near the foot of the San Gabriel Mountains, the municipal building anchored the Pasadena Civic Center. Influenced by sixteenth-century Italian architect Andrea Palladio, the team

Above left: Restored arcade. *Above right:* Entry. Both images courtesy of Architectural Resources Group. *Opposite:* View from Euclid Avenue (east elevation). Image © victormuschettophotography.com.

Renovated historic Council Chambers. Image © victormuschettophotography.com.

designed a rectangular building with a six-story circular tower. Construction began in January 1926 and required more than one million board feet of lumber, twenty thousand cubic yards of concrete, and more than thirty-five thousand tons of rock and gravel from the San Gabriel River. Craftsmen used Alaskan marble, cast stone, wrought iron, copper, vertical-grained white oak, and Cordova clay roof tiles. Its 235 rooms and passageways cover 170,000 square feet. Construction cost $1.34 million at the time.

For seventy years, Pasadena City Hall was the city's most treasured landmark. But by the 1990s, studies showed that a major earthquake would destroy much of the building. While it seemed to be in good condition, closer inspection revealed decaying stonework,

water damage, and deep cracks within two of the hall's stair towers and in the lantern in the large dome. The structure also did not comply with the Americans with Disabilities Act, and its outdated mechanical, electrical, and safety systems needed replacement.

After years of debate, city officials decided to protect the historic structure using seismic base-isolation technology. The original basement floor slab was removed, a new foundation was excavated and installed, a basement floor transfer system was put in place, and 240 friction-pendulum isolators were installed. The ten-year rehabilitation project also completely restored the structure's exterior plaster and cast-stone facade details, as well as all the building's marble, quarry tile, light fixtures, wood doors, and other woodwork.

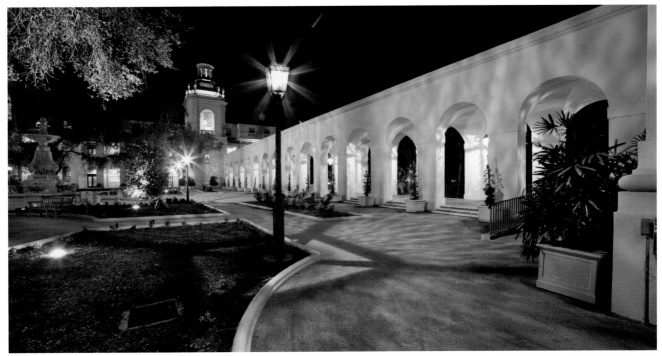

Courtyard and reconstructed arcade. Image © victormuschettophotography.com.

The city had debated whether it could afford the $117 million project when there were so many competing interests—education, public safety, parks, housing. At the time, the editorial page of the *Pasadena Sun* urged the city to avoid "lily-gilding," but not at the expense of the landmark. "Yes, the human needs are great in Pasadena," the editorial stated. "But there is an undeniable and undeniably practical need to keep the city and its symbols great so that our descendants can take pride in the City Beautiful as well."

BUILT: 1927

AWARDED: 2008

OWNER: City of Pasadena, Martin Pastucha, Director of Public Works

ORIGINAL ARCHITECT: Bakewell and Brown

PRIME ARCHITECT AND CONSERVATOR: Architectural Resources Group, Inc., Bruce Judd, FAIA, and Susan McDonald

HISTORIC PRESERVATION/FEMA MONITOR: Historic Resources Group, Peyton Hall, FAIA

STRUCTURAL ENGINEER: Forell/Elsesser Engineers, Inc., Steve Marusich

GENERAL CONTRACTOR: Clark Construction

TEMPLE SHERITH ISRAEL SAN FRANCISCO

WHEN SAN FRANCISCO'S Sherith Israel reopened in 2011, the congregation held a foot-stomping bluegrass concert led by financier Warren Hellman and his band, the Wronglers. The event—billed Hardly Strictly Shabbat after the Hardly Strictly Bluegrass festival that Hellman put on each fall in Golden Gate Park—was perhaps not a traditional way for a synagogue to mark the end of a construction project. But it was typical of the freewheeling Sherith Israel.

Jews started arriving in San Francisco in significant numbers during the Gold Rush. Like other immigrant communities, the newcomers were eager to establish religious institutions. In September 1849, Jews gathered in a wood-framed tent and did their best to celebrate Rosh Hashanah and Yom Kippur without the help of a rabbi. By the next year's Passover and High Holy Days, they were more organized, forming benevolent societies and buying land in the Mission District for a cemetery. Two congregations emerged—Sherith Israel and Emanu-El.

In September of 1905, after losing two synagogues to fire and outgrowing two more, Sherith Israel consecrated its new home at California and Webster Streets. Designed by Albert Pissis, the grand domed building

All images © David Wakely.

is a fusion of Byzantine and Romanesque forms, heavily influenced by the architect's Beaux-Arts training. The building cost $250,000 and stood 140 feet above California Street. Its sanctuary contained 3,500 organ pipes, 1,400 seats, 1,109 decorative lightbulbs, 89 ornamental leaded-glass windows, and 32 arched clear-glass windows in its outer drum. With its opalescent stained glass, stencil frescoes, and Honduran mahogany woodwork, Sherith Israel was immediately hailed as the most impressive temple west of Chicago.

Rabbi Jacob Nieto cautioned his flock not to let it go to their heads. "Beauty should not be a distraction from more important things like prayer and the spectacle of poverty, which exists in our midst," he said. After the earthquake and fire of 1906, the synagogue was the largest structure still standing in the city, spared by the fact that the blaze that swallowed up most of the city stopped at Van Ness Avenue. For two years the synagogue was the home of the San Francisco Superior Court and the scene of the corruption trials of San Francisco Mayor Eugene Schmitz and boss Abe Ruef.

While the synagogue held up equally well during the 1989 Loma Prieta earthquake, city building inspectors were less forgiving. As a public building with unreinforced masonry walls, Sherith Israel faced a tough choice: either complete an expensive seismic upgrade or shut its doors. After a heroic fundraising campaign and decades of studies, the engineering team settled on a "center coring" method that would strengthen the structure without damaging its historical integrity. Workers drilled 130 vertical "tunnels" from the synagogue's parapet through the sandstone blocks down to the foundation, dropped steel rods into the openings, and then poured in polyester resin. The salmon-hued exterior coating was also removed, much to everyone's delight.

The renovation, led by real-estate consultant Lynn Sedway, included the restoration of the five prophet windows lining the foyer as well as the one-thousand-pound rose window overlooking California Street. The windows were shipped to a stained-glass studio in Milton, Iowa. "Someone said the cleaning up of the prophet windows was like going from analog TV to high-definition," said Craig Etlin, chairman of the synagogue's building committee. Sherith Israel's most famous stained-glass window also got a facelift. The great arched west window depicts Moses not at Mount Sinai but at Yosemite's Half Dome. "Remember, for those who came west, California was the promised land," said Sedway.

BUILT: 1905

AWARDED: 2011

OWNER: Congregation Sherith Israel, Leslie Kane

ORIGINAL ARCHITECT: Albert Pissis

ARCHITECT: ELS Architecture and Urban Design, Kurt Schindler

HISTORIC PRESERVATION CONSULTANT: Wiss, Janney, Elstner Associates, Inc., Alan Dreyfuss

SEISMIC DESIGN ENGINEER: Wiss, Janney, Elstner Associates, Inc., Terrence Paret

GENERAL CONTRACTOR: Plant Construction, Dylan Berry

SANTA FE DEPOT FRESNO

WHEN IT OPENED IN 1899 the Santa Fe train station in Fresno was celebrated less for its architectural merits than for the impact local farmers hoped it would have on business. The Mission Revival station was a busy stopping point for what was then a new San Francisco and San Joaquin Valley Railroad. For years farmers had complained that the Southern Pacific Railroad, known as "The Octopus," had a monopoly on local railroad business and overcharged the Central Valley farmers and travelers relying on its trains. The new railroad station "marked the beginning of an era of development and prosperity for the San Joaquin Valley in general and Fresno County in particular," stated an editorial in the *Fresno Republican*. "The Octopus, whose tentacles

Above left: East side arches after restoration, 2005. *Above right:* East entry after restoration, 2005. *Opposite:* Northwest corner after restoration, 2005. All images © Keith Seaman Photography.

have strangled commerce, industry and agriculture in this great basin has been deprived of its power to do any further harm," the *Republican* stated.

The Santa Fe Depot stretched long and narrow along the dusty tracks. It was classic Mission Revival—arched doors and windows, a hipped-tiled roof, a single tower, and several turrets, all capped with pyramidal tiled roofs. A terrazzo floor and wood-paneled walls greeted travelers, who were ushered into cozy separate men's and women's waiting rooms, each with a working fireplace.

Fresno was a busy shipping point and also served as the railroad company's Valley Division headquarters, so almost as soon as the depot was finished, the railroad company started altering it. Nine separate modification projects took place between 1909 and 1985. The depot's south wing was expanded, its outdoor waiting room enclosed. Finally, in 1966 the station was shut to passenger use and the waiting room converted to a communications center for the railroad. For forty years Amtrak train passengers alighting in Fresno were welcomed not by the grand station but by an indistinct two-story building with Coke machines and metal folding chairs. "It was not a good front door for Fresno," said project architect Chris Johnson, who fought for the building's preservation.

Meanwhile, next door the Santa Fe Railroad Depot sat ignored. The clock tower was concealed by ductwork. The original waiting rooms were a rat's nest of cramped offices and storage space. The terrazzo floor was hidden under concrete; plaster covered the waiting-room fireplaces. "It was broken up into little spaces—you couldn't tell you were in the depot," said Johnson.

The city took over the property in 2003 with the intention of restoring it, but the project stalled, and Amtrak proposed replacing the depot with a new building. In the end, the renovation prevailed only because it was cheaper. The $6 million project returned the depot to its 1899 appearance. The depot's walls and roofs were seismically strengthened, the tower and clock were reconstructed, and windows and doors were rebuilt or replaced. The construction team stripped ten layers of white paint from the brick fireplaces in the waiting rooms. The concrete floor was blasted off to expose the original sections of the worn-out terrazzo floor. "You can feel the presence of people a hundred years ago impatiently scuffing their boots while waiting at the ticket counter," said Johnson.

Today the station is the tenth busiest of Amtrak's seventy-two California stations, with nearly one thousand passengers a day. On a recent spring day a group of four retired friends from the North Fork Women's Club were exploring the old station and getting ready to take a little train ride to historic Hanford, a half hour to the south. What's in Hanford? they were asked. "Superior Dairy," said Donna Hardy. "Ice cream. Peach. Lemon in the summer."

BUILT: 1899

AWARDED: 2005

ORIGINAL ARCHITECT:
William Benson Storey

PRINCIPAL AND PROJECT
LEAD: Johnson Architecture,
Christopher A. Johnson, AIA

HISTORIC PRESERVATION
CONSULTANT: Heritage
Architecture & Planning, Brian
Rickling

LEAD ENGINEER:
Structural Focus, David Cocke

GENERAL CONTRACTOR:
Reyman Brothers Construction,
Jace Callendar

HEARST MEMORIAL MINING BUILDING BERKELEY

IN 1896 PHOEBE APPERSON HEARST wrote the University of California Board of Regents pledging her support for a new campus in Berkeley. "I desire to say," wrote Hearst, "that the success of this enterprise shall not be hampered in any way by a money consideration." She was true to her word. The widow of senator and mining millionaire George R. Hearst, she bankrolled the UC Berkeley campus master plan, an architecture competition, and a center for the College of Mining

named for her husband. He was, she said, "a plain, honest man and a good miner."

And in the Hearst Memorial Mining Building, Phoebe Hearst built her late husband quite a monument. Designed by John Galen Howard, the academic building is part Beaux-Arts magnificence and part rough-and-tumble research laboratory. It served a discipline that was both dirty and dangerous—and it reflected that fact. In a four-story atrium lab space,

Above and opposite: Images © 2002 Tim Griffith. *Previous page:* Restored central atrium and graduate student work space, 2002. Image © Tim Griffith.

students learned how to build and operate mines; they studied the science of digging, lighting, and ventilating deep vertical airshafts. Along with desks and chalkboards, the building was equipped with smelters, rock crushers, drill rigs, and fume hoods.

The building's centerpiece, the grand three-story Memorial Hall, resembles a mineshaft, with exposed steel lattice columns and trusses, and Guastavino arches—a self-supporting arch system that uses interlocking terra-cotta tiles set in mortar. A trio of twenty-four-foot-wide steel circular skylights illuminates the ceiling, while the lobby's globe lights twinkle at dusk. The building's exterior is Sierra White granite; its staircases are marble. On the front facade of the building, six straining human figures—Howard said they represented the "the primal elements"—shoulder heavy

redwood brackets to support the red-tile roof. Howard said mining was "a ruthless assault upon the bowels of the world, a contest with the crudest and most rudimentary forces...and its expression in architecture must, to be true, have something of the rude, the Cyclopean."

Over the decades, studies in the Hearst Memorial Mining Building evolved from mining to mineral engineering to the latest in materials science and nanotechnology. But while the study program prospered, the building became a relic. Brick floors in the Mining Hall were covered up in linoleum to protect them against foot traffic. In 1947 the university filled two interior light wells with bathrooms and hallways. The four-story central atrium was converted to office space. "The building was an absolute mess," said Brendan Kelly, who was a project architect with NBBJ Architects. "There were labs [in which] if the lights went out it would have taken you a week to find your way out."

The Hearst Memorial Mining Building sits just eight hundred feet west of the Hayward Fault. Faced with the need to seismically stabilize the building, engineers determined that the building deserved nothing less than the least obtrusive (and most expensive) solution: a base-isolation system. The sixty-million-pound landmark was severed from its foundation, lifted eleven feet into the air, and then lowered onto one hundred thirty-four squat rubber barrels that isolate the building from an earthquake's destructive back-and-forth movement.

The retrofit allowed the design and construction team to bring the building back to its original form. Inside, the light courts and atrium were opened up. The battleship linoleum was removed from the Mining Hall, revealing buff brick floors. According to Scott Shackleton, the university's assistant dean for facilities and capital projects, the adhesive holding the linoleum was so thick that workers had to break into the surface layer of brick to get it off. Even with fifteen coats of sealant, the floors remain porous: "We have to be very careful when people spill their red wine—the bricks want to suck that stuff up."

BUILT: 1907

AWARDED: 2003

OWNER: University of California, Berkeley, Rob Gayle, Assistant Vice-Chancellor

ARCHITECT & PROJECT LEAD: NBBJ, Brendan Kelly

ORIGINAL ARCHITECT: John Galen Howard

HISTORIC PRESERVATION CONSULTANT: Page & Turnbull, J. Gordon Turnbull, FAIA

LEAD ENGINEER: Rutherford & Chekene, Harold Davis, Principal-in-Charge

COLORADO STREET BRIDGE PASADENA

THE EPICENTER OF THE 1989 Loma Prieta earthquake was 380 miles from Pasadena's Colorado Street Bridge, but that doesn't mean it wasn't felt there. When the quake hit, Pasadena moved swiftly to close the 1913 bridge to vehicular traffic. The Northern California quake had sent a 230-ton section of the Bay Bridge's upper deck slamming down on the lower deck like a trapdoor, killing a motorist. The possibility that something similar could happen in Pasadena was a chance officials weren't willing to take.

For Pasadena Heritage, the preservation group that had spent a dozen years fighting to preserve the Art Deco bridge, it was a horrifying development. "Everybody thought, 'Oh my God, what will the result be?'" said Sue Mossman, executive director of Pasadena Heritage.

The Colorado Street Bridge was the tallest concrete bridge of its day, and the first curvilinear bridge ever designed. With eleven arches, the bridge marches one hundred fifty feet above the broad, rocky Arroyo

Above and previous page: Images courtesy of Parsons Corporation.

Seco—the name means "dry wash" in Spanish—a wide riverbed that is a tributary of the Los Angeles River.

The bridge connected Pasadena to Los Angeles at a time when automobile sales were exploding; Pasadena had the highest percentage of car ownership in the country with four thousand cars for fifty thousand residents. Yet without a bridge to cross the Arroyo Seco, motorists had to go far to the north or the south. The alternative was descending the steep eastern slope by horse and wagon, crossing a bridge over the stream, and then climbing the west bank through Eagle Rock Pass.

Given this harsh topography, the bridge was a challenge to build. Construction took eighteen months. Solid footing eluded engineers in the seasonally wet arroyo bed. Horse carts hauled materials down the steep sides of the gorge—some eleven thousand cubic yards of concrete and six hundred tons of steel. Gravel for the concrete was dug from hillsides of the arroyo. Three men were killed building the bridge. "The engineers had enormous challenges, but they rose to them with extraordinary talent and guts," said Mossman.

But it wasn't long before some felt the bridge was obsolete. As early as 1935 there was a proposal to knock it down to make way for a freeway. In 1951 the wrecking ball hovered again when plans for the Foothill Freeway became a reality. A public outcry saved the bridge.

When Pasadena Heritage was founded in 1978 the bridge was in disrepair. It remained a structurally sound regional transportation link, but cosmetically it was crumbling. The five-globe cast-iron Art Deco lights had been replaced with single globes. The ornate

Grand opening of the restored bridge in December 1993. Image courtesy of Parsons Corporation.

balustrades were removed when barriers to deter jumpers were erected. (Still called "the Suicide Bridge" by many, the span was a particularly popular place to commit suicide during the Great Depression.) After Loma Prieta, Pasadena Heritage fought a movement to leave it standing but not allow vehicles to use it.

Eventually, a coalition led by Heritage and the Pasadena Department of Public Works put together the $24 million needed to both make the bridge safe and restore its original lighting standards, balustrades, and romantic seating bays that punctuate its sidewalk. Today, every other year Pasadena Heritage holds a fundraiser celebration on the bridge that attracts four thousand people. Mossman said her favorite time of day to walk across the bridge is at dusk, as darkness settles on the Arroyo Seco and as the cast-iron lamps with their grape-like clusters of bulbs flicker on. "It was always an icon, but it has become a reembraced icon, as something not only historic and beautiful but also something that was saved," said Mossman.

BUILT: 1913

AWARDED: 1994

OWNER: City of Pasadena

ORIGINAL ARCHITECT: Unknown

ENGINEER: Parsons De Leuw, Inc. (now called Parsons Corporation)

ENGINEER: Melvyn Green and Associates, Melvyn Green, SE

FRIENDSHIP BAPTIST CHURCH PASADENA

PASADENA HAS CHANGED, but the Friendship Baptist Church has not. All around the stately church, boxy condos have popped up in stucco pastels. The African American community once concentrated in the neighborhood has dispersed to northern Pasadena and elsewhere. The brick warehouses in the old working-class neighborhood have been refurbished into the offices of architects, bistros, and social-media companies. But Pasadena's oldest African American

church has stood its ground on West Dayton Street. It serves the same purpose it did in February of 1960, when Martin Luther King Jr. preached from its pulpit. "They tried to condemn us back in '94, but we weren't going for that," said building manager Harry Hudson, who was baptized at the church in 1944.

Friendship Baptist Church was founded in September 1893. It was the first African American Baptist Church in Pasadena, and for many years it was the biggest. But by the 1920s the congregation had outgrown its home, and Reverend W. H. Tillman led the members to acquire a new site and erect the present building. Old photographs show church ladies sitting on folding chairs next to the construction site, fanning themselves with hymnbooks. Designed by Norman Foote Marsh, the nineteen-thousand-square-foot church combined Spanish Colonial Revival and Mission styles. A bell tower rises from the corner of the three-story structure, and a Mission portico leads to the back wing. Lit by stained-glass windows, the sanctuary and chapel have dark oak trim, pews, and doors.

After the church was severely damaged in the 1994 Northridge earthquake, building officials ordered it closed. The congregation sought refuge in a school gym, then a warehouse. Under the direction of Reverend Lucious Smith, the restoration included reestablishing original color schemes and cast-stone finishes on the exterior. The woodwork and the stained-glass windows were refurbished. The heating and electrical systems were brought up to modern standards. There is now air-conditioning—something that is especially appreciated on summer Sundays when the sanctuary has a spillover crowd.

Above and opposite: Images © Tavo Olmos, Photographer.

With the building on solid footing, the congregation can focus on its Christian mission. These days, Sunday school and youth ministry rooms are being used as temporary shelter for homeless families. Air mattresses, cribs, stuffed animals, and plastic Tonka trucks furnish rooms labeled "God's Squad" and "Youth Department."

"We have fourteen people staying here, nine kids," said Hudson. "They all lost their homes to fore-closure. Some lost their jobs. That is the way it goes. We help people. Help them get on their feet, get an apartment—stuff like that. Keep them nice and warm."

BUILT: 1925

AWARDED: 2000

OWNER: Friendship Baptist Church, Clifton Valentine, President/Treasurer

ORIGINAL ARCHITECT:
Norman Foote Marsh

PROJECT LEAD ARCHITECT,
HISTORICAL ARCHITECT:
M2A Milofsky & Michali
Architects, Thomas Michali

LEAD ENGINEER:
Krakower & Associates, Michael Krakower

GENERAL CONTRACTOR:
Mark Sauer Construction, Inc., Mark Sauer

Both images courtesy of M2A Milofsky, Michali and Cox Architects.

RICHMOND MEMORIAL CIVIC CENTER RICHMOND

THE LONG DECLINE AND rebirth of the Richmond Civic Center is the story of a hard-luck-fallen industrial powerhouse with a lot of heart. The three-building U-shaped civic-center complex—which originally included an auditorium, hall of justice, and city hall—was conceived of by architects Richard Neutra and R. M. Schindler and then later designed by one of San Francisco's most famous civic architects, Timothy L. Pflueger. The complex exuded the confidence of a prosperous and forward-thinking industrial center, the swagger of a mighty city that churned out ships, tanks, and Ford automobiles on its busy waterfront.

Upon completion in 1948 the center complex exemplified civic modernism. It was pure, linear, transparent, concise, and open. Its long, thin bricks were uniform in size, pattern, and color. A prominent colonnade ringed all three buildings, tying the narrow forms together and lifting the structures off the ground.

But Richmond's industrial economy fell sharply after the war, as first the shipyards closed up and then the Ford Assembly Plant moved to a suburb of San Jose. Unemployment spiked, and the makeshift bunkers thrown together to house shipyard workers were beset by poverty and crime. By the time the Loma Prieta earthquake hit in 1989, the once-proud civic center stood neglected amid residential streets of auto shops and boarded-up buildings with couches in the front yards. The basement of the civic center flooded, and the grassy plaza in front of the complex resembled a muddy football field at the end of the season. The city government said farewell to the seismically unsafe building and moved to a concrete, fluorescent-lit tilt-up building in an industrial park on Harbor Way.

Richmond didn't have the money to rebuild the old civic center—and wasn't sure it was a worthwhile investment. "The City of Richmond was on the verge of bankruptcy and they went through an enormous amount of debate: Do you give up on this thing, knock it down and forget it? Or do you come back and reinvest in it?" said project manager Mark Kelley.

In the end, Richmond decided it would not turn its back on the old civic center. This coincided with a strong—but short-lived—housing boom, which generated enough money to bankroll its preservation. Large portions of the existing walls, floors, and ceilings were reused to preserve much of the original structure. The construction team sourced bricks from the same Folsom manufacturer that had provided the originals. New terrazzo flooring replicated what was there before. The former Hall of Justice now houses a variety of city

Above and previous page: City Hall, 2009. Image © Vam Y.K. Cheung.

Restored auditorium lobby. Image © Vam Y. K. Cheung.

offices. On the west is the Memorial Auditorium—a venue that has hosted everything from roller derbies to senior proms. "Our vision for this project was to bring critical city administrative functions back to downtown while also reviving the central business district and honoring the original architecture," said project architect Michael Walden of Nadel Architects.

Chad Smalley, who works on redevelopment issues in the city, loves the complex so much he took pictures of his copper 1947 Plymouth parked in front. The building and the car look like kindred spirits. "It's not as intrusive as some buildings I have been in where you know you are in a shell of another building. This one seems more integrated than a bunch of retrofitted buildings," he said.

BUILT: 1948

AWARDED: 2010

ORIGINAL ARCHITECT: Milton Pflueger

CEDA DIRECTOR/PROJECT EXECUTIVE: City of Richmond, Steve Duran

STRUCTURAL ENGINEER: The KPA Group, Hratch Kouyoumdjian

DEVELOPER: Alliance Property Group, Harley Searcy, Danielle Curls Bennett, and Kipling Sheppard (Wasatch Advantage Group)

ARCHITECT: Nadel Architecture, Michael Walden, AIA, Michael Rominske, and Rhoden Skyles

CONSTRUCTION MANAGER: Mack 5, Mark Kelley

GENERAL CONTRACTOR: Charles Pankow Builders, LLC, Brett Firebaugh

Restored lobby. Image © Vam Y. K. Cheung.

FIRST CHURCH OF CHRIST, SCIENTIST SAN DIEGO

WHETHER TO RETAIN or raze one of San Diego's greatest early modernist buildings came down to a vote. In 1991 the congregation of the 1,200-seat First Church of Christ, Scientist, gathered to decide whether their church, designed in 1910 by Irving Gill, would be restored or replaced with a new building.

It had not been a good run for Gill or the church, perched on Bankers Hill overlooking the Pacific. A 1950s redesign had removed many of the most distinctive features, and a dome that had been sealed during World War II as a precaution against enemy aircraft

was never reopened. Many other architectural details had been covered up: arches, arched windows, and a pipe organ. By the time the congregation was debating the fate of the church, many of Gill's best buildings, including the Klauber and Timken houses in San Diego and the Dodge house in Los Angeles, had been knocked down. In the 1950s and 1960s, critics and historians largely overlooked Gill's work.

Keeping far from the center of the architecture world in the European capitals, Gill was an artist with the confidence of conviction. His work, often compared to the work of the Austrian patriarch of modernism, Adolf Loos, was very different from the historicist and richly decorated work favored in San Francisco and Los Angeles at the time. Raised a Quaker, Gill gravitated to a simplified palette, eliminating unnecessary details. He preferred concrete floors to wood because they wouldn't be as attractive to insects or rodents. He liked doorjambs and cabinets flush to the walls so as not to catch dust. He designed easily maintained, sanitary homes with a bent toward purity. Gill discussed his ideal of simplicity in his 1916 essay, "The New Architecture of the West." In the essay he wrote that the "source of all architectural strength" emerged from the "straight line, the arch, the cube, and the circle in combination.... Every artist must sooner or later reckon directly, personally, with these four principles."

The First Church of Christ, Scientist, embodied all four of those strengths in its lengthy arcade, blunt tower, and glass dome. Instead of lining up the pews on a vertical axis, Gill created a long horizontal axis,

Above left: Looking toward the pulpit, with the stained-glass dome visible, 2000. *Above right*: Interior, 2000. Both images courtesy of Kelley-Markham Architecture. *Previous page*: Contextual view, 2000. Image © John Durant, Kelley-Markham Architecture.

giving the space a more democratic feeling. Rows of ground-floor arches on the north and east sides of the building and second-floor arches on the south side of the building drew light into the auditorium. In the *Los Angeles Times,* historian Kevin Starr suggested that Gill's design exemplified "a certain collective and redemptive progressivism....It can be argued that Gill—in his autodidactism, his refusal to be intimidated before history and tradition, his capacity for the direct and powerful line—paralleled what his Northern California contemporary Jack London was simultaneously trying to do with literature."

Bruce Coombs, executive director of Save Our Heritage Organization, said the 1992 restoration preserved more than a building: also the reputation of a great architect. "It was a major restoration of the largest work of an architect who hasn't always been treated very well," he said.

Exterior arches, 2000. Image © John Durant, Kelley-Markham Architecture.

BUILT: 1910

AWARDED: 2002

OWNER: First Church of Christ, Scientist

ORIGINAL ARCHITECT: Irving Gill

ARCHITECT: Kelley-Markham Architecture & Planning, Jim Kelley-Markham

HISTORIC PRESERVATION CONSULTANT: Kathleen Kelley-Markham

CONSULTING ENGINEER: Kariotis & Associates, John Kariotis

GENERAL CONTRACTOR: Tony Wanket Construction, Tony Wanket

CONSERVATORY OF FLOWERS SAN FRANCISCO

SEEN FROM A DISTANCE, the whitewashed Conservatory of Flowers seems to spread its wings like a great egret against Golden Gate Park's rolling lawns; you half expect the luminous structure to rise and vanish into the Richmond District fog. But what seems ethereal and dreamlike from afar is actually one of San Francisco's oldest treasures. For more than 130 years,

the glass-and-wood greenhouse, the oldest of its kind in the United States, has transported visitors to the humid rain forests of Central America, South America, and Southeast Asia.

The conservatory is so unusual because it was designed not as a public building but to satisfy the eccentricities of real-estate mogul James Lick. Other large public

Above left: View from the interior of the lower dome following 1995 winter storm damage. *Above right:* The dome is lifted into place during the restoration phase. Both images courtesy of Architectural Resources Group. *Opposite:* Image © David Wakely.

conservatories, like Longwood Gardens in Philadelphia and the Haupt Conservatory in New York, were constructed out of cast iron or steel. Lick, who had made a killing buying San Francisco land before the gold rush, ordered his conservatory made out of wood. Already in his seventies, the amateur botanist was probably not too concerned with longevity. He wanted a quiet place to raise tropical plants at his Santa Clara estate between the Guadalupe River and Saratoga Creek.

But it was not to be. Lick died in 1876, not long after the arrival of the crates holding the prefabricated conservatory building materials. In 1877 Lick's estate sold the materials to a group of twenty-seven San Francisco businessmen, who bequeathed them to the city's Park Commission for construction in Golden Gate Park. The conservatory opened in 1879: 250 feet long and 55 feet tall with 16,800 glass panes held together with 2 tons of putty.

For all its beauty, however, the building was fickle from the start. In 1883 a boiler explosion destroyed the main dome. From 1933 to 1946 the building was closed due to structural instability. Finally, in 1995, in what seemed to be a knockout blow, a windstorm howled through the fragile glass house, leaving in its wake shattered glass tiles and splintered arches. The postmortem reports on the wreckage were not hopeful. When the engineers and architects dissected the arches in the main building, they found that the old-growth redwood was riddled with holes from the original square nails, and that decades of extreme moisture had rotted out the frame.

After a seven-year, $25 million reconstruction process championed by First Lady Hillary Rodham Clinton, the building reopened in 2003. Today it attracts more than two million visitors a year, and many locals return again and again. Terry Nevin, who remembers throwing pennies in the water-lilies pool as a five-year-old, today brings her grandchildren there. "It's a

Above and opposite: Both images © David Wakely.

magical place for me," says Nevin, adding that tossing coins in the water is now frowned upon.

But much remains mysterious, even to those who rebuilt the conservatory. For example: where did it really come from? Some claim the kit was shipped from France; others say England or Ireland. But project manager Debbie Cooper of Architectural Resources Group thinks it is more likely a California original. When the building was dissected, the work crew found that the main arches were redwood; the mullions, pine; and the purloins, Douglas fir. All are California woods.

Restored pond room. Image © David Wakely.

BUILT: 1879

AWARDED: 2005

ORIGINAL ARCHITECT: Unknown

EXECUTIVE DIRECTOR:
Conservatory of Flowers,
Scot Medbury

PRINCIPAL: Architectural
Resources Group, Inc., Bruce
Judd, FAIA

STRUCTURAL ENGINEER:
Tennebaum-Manheim Engineers

GENERAL CONTRACTOR:
ISEC/Troy's Contracting

ALCATRAZ HISTORIC GARDENS SAN FRANCISCO

ALCATRAZ WILL NEVER BE most famous for its flora and fauna. After all, George "Machine Gun Kelly" Barnes never tended the roses of Alcatraz. Nor did Al Capone or Boston mobster Whitey Bulger, who was locked up on the Rock from 1959 to 1962. Yet on this twenty-two-acre outcropping a mile and a half from downtown San Francisco is an improbable garden as fascinating as any of the criminals who resided there.

Alcatraz was first documented in 1775 by Spaniard Juan Manuel de Ayala, who named the island *La Isla de los Alcatraces,* or "the Island of the Pelicans." It became an army fortress in the 1800s and a military prison in 1861;

Above: Officers' Row Gardens after clearing and replanting, 2009. *Previous page:* West Road border after rehabilitation, 2009. Both images courtesy of Golden Gate National Parks Conservancy and The Garden Conservancy.

Above: Rose Garden before rehabilitation (2005) and after (2009), with restored historic paths and railings. Both images courtesy of Golden Gate National Parks Conservancy and The Garden Conservancy.

from 1934 to 1963 it was a federal penitentiary. Today Alcatraz is part of the National Park Service's Golden Gate National Recreation Area.

Military inmates started working in the gardens long before the island was a federal penitentiary. When the Federal Bureau of Prisons took control in 1933, Freddie Reichel, the first secretary to Warden James Johnson, knew he would need help from inmates if he were to maintain the gardens. At first, Johnson was reluctant to let the inmates loose among the flowers. Finally, "after much heckling on my part," Reichel convinced him otherwise, according to a 1933 letter he wrote to the California Horticultural Society. The first inmate assigned to the job was picked not for his gardening abilities but because "the other residents would have nothing to do with him." Reichel found his new helper

Officers' Row Gardens before rehabilitation (left, 2005 and 2006) and after (2009). Images courtesy of Golden Gate National Parks Conservancy and The Garden Conservancy.

"certainly no mastermind," but gave him an "easy-to-manage subject: gladiolus."

Eventually, Reichel enlisted two other gardeners. Inmates Elliott Michener and Dick Franseen, both convicted counterfeiters, cultivated bell roses and delphiniums under the watch of the tower gunners "seven days a week." After they were released from Alcatraz, Franseen and Michener went professional, working as gardeners together at Quality Park Farms in Wisconsin. Michener missed Alcatraz—or at least its flowers. He wrote Warden Edwin Swope and requested a "bush of our 'Gardener rose'" be sent to his place of work.

When the federal government abandoned Alcatraz in 1963, no one stayed behind to deadhead. Plants unable to survive without maintenance vanished, while others spread like fire. Blackberries, ivy, and honeysuckle went wild. Soon, it was no longer obvious that the island had been planted and once lovingly maintained.

In 2003 the Garden Conservancy and Golden Gate National Parks Conservancy formed a partnership to resurrect the gardens. Using photos and letters, mostly from the penitentiary era, they rehabilitated what they could. Buried under forty years of plant debris were the bones of the garden: its terraces, paths, railings, and foundations. Plants that had been buried began to flourish after removal of invasive species. Cape tulips popped up in the rose terrace. There were ten different species of surviving roses, including *Rosa* Bardou Job, a wine-red climber so rare that the Welsh Museum of Life had been looking for it for years. (Eventually a cutting was sent to Wales, where it is known as the Al Capone Rose.)

Volunteers have logged more than thirty thousand hours in the gardens. They turn up black rubber balls that had bounced over the wall during inmate handball games. They have found old spoons folded in half (intended as weapons), brass buttons, fuel cans, and rifle casings from a 1946 riot when marines opened fire on the island. "There is always treasure," says volunteer Dick Minor. A retired biologist, Minor is known as the "Worm Man of Alcatraz" because of his dedication to composting. He is proud that 99 percent of the garden waste is composted. He thinks the inmate gardeners were way ahead of their time in terms of sustainable horticulture. "[Reichel] had a sense of sustainability without knowing much about it."

<table>
<tr><td>BUILT: N/A</td><td>PROJECTS COORDINATOR:
Golden Gate National Parks
Conservancy, David Dusterhoff</td><td>PRESERVATION PROJECTS
SPECIALIST: The Garden
Conservancy, Elizabeth Byers,
Consultant</td></tr>
<tr><td>AWARDED: 2009</td><td></td><td></td></tr>
<tr><td>ORIGINAL ARCHITECT: N/A</td><td>CO-PROJECT LEAD, PROJECTS
DIRECTOR: The Garden
Conservancy, William Noble</td><td>LANDSCAPE CONTRACTOR:
Lafayette Landscaping, Dean
Lafayette</td></tr>
</table>

POINT SUR LIGHTHOUSE BIG SUR

FOR MORE THAN EIGHTY years, starting in 1889, the merchant marines and fishermen plying California's Central Coast had a dependable ally at Point Sur: an eighteen-foot-tall Fresnel lens that flashed white and red every fifteen seconds. At night its beam blasted through sixteen panels of prisms and lit up the corners of a craggy coastline. When it was foggy, the twin steam whistles honked every thirty-five seconds.

After numerous shipwrecks in the area, in 1886 Congress finally allocated $50,000 to construct a light station at Point Sur to fill a dangerous gap between already existing lighthouses at Piedras Blancas and Pigeon Point. Point Sur is a steep mound of volcanic rock connected by a low bridge of land—a tombolo—to the rocky Big Sur coast. Three hundred sixty feet high, it seems to have broken away from the coastal mountains and run aground. The apex of the rock was blasted to create a flat area to build on. A tramway flanked by a wooden stairway was built on the eastern side of the rock to haul materials to the summit. Logs and granite

Above left and right: Lighthouse after restoration, 2002. Both images © Robert Carver, Carver & Schicketanz Architects. *Opposite*: Point Sur with lighthouse (right). Image courtesy of Carver & Schicketanz Architects.

stones for the buildings were cut and quarried from the Big Sur hills. The lighthouse was only part of a little village needed to run the station. A barn sheltered horses and cattle. A carpentry and blacksmith shop held tools. A three-story granite triplex on the southern end of the rock housed three keepers and their families. The centerpiece was the lighthouse's light itself, a first-order Fresnel lens, manufactured by Barbier & Fenestre of Paris. The 4,330-pound lens was assembled in the lantern room, where a kerosene lantern illuminated it for the first time on August 1, 1889.

The keepers lived an isolated life. They had small vegetable gardens atop the rock; other supplies arrived aboard a lighthouse tender every four months. Supplies were placed in cargo nets and hoisted from skiffs to the wharf, where they were packed into railway cars and winched to the top of the station. By the 1960s the US Coast Guard, which had taken over Point Sur in 1939, started automating light stations to save money. In 1974 the last Point Sur keeper packed up and left. The buildings were boarded up. The Fresnel lens, replaced by an aero beacon, was sent to the Allen Knight Maritime Museum of Monterey.

With nobody to paint it, the lantern room started to rust and corrode, its noncompatible metals eating themselves up. Water seeped into the tower when it rained. A bullet hole pierced the cupola. The wooden floorboards in the other buildings rotted away as water rats took up residence on the property. The decaying structures prompted the formation of the Central Coast Lighthouse Keepers, who began to lobby to save the station. "I believe we caught it just in time," said Robert Carver, who was the project architect and involved in the lighthouse group.

A total restoration of the light station, led by International Chimney Corporation and a band of volunteers, was completed in 2001; the buildings are now open to the public. Poets gather at the lighthouse under the moonlight to read the work of Robinson Jeffers, whose poems eulogize the Central Coast. Volunteer Doug Williams works at the light station every Thursday with a crew of fellow retirees—mostly ex-military and former contractors. Sitting on the west side of the light station and looking both ways along the coast, you could be back in 1890, he says. "The fog is fickle—it comes in quickly and vanishes as fast," said Williams.

BUILT: 1889

AWARDED: 2004

OWNER: CCLK Chairman, Douglas Williams

ORIGINAL ARCHITECT: Unknown

ARCHITECT: Carver & Schicketanz Architects; Robert Carver, Principal, and Libby Barnes, Staff Architect

HISTORIC PRESERVATION CONSULTANT: Architectural Conservation, Molly Lambert

LEAD ENGINEER: Shoreline Engineering, Bruce Elster

CONTRACTOR: International Chimney Corporation, Ron Upliniger

Restored staircase, 2002. Image © Robert Carver, Carver & Schicketanz Architects.

MANZANAR GUARD TOWER INDEPENDENCE

BARBED WIRE STRETCHES ALONG Highway 395 as far as the eye can see, an ordinary fence amid arid land and sagebrush fields that could easily have been erected by a rancher to keep cattle from wandering off. It is not until you reach the far east side of the frontage road that you see a four-story, weathered wooden guard tower. Then, if you know anything about the area, you realize you are not skirting a normal California ranch:

you are at Manzanar, the former internment camp where ten thousand Japanese Americans were held against their will during World War II.

In 1995 the National Park Service and the non-profit Friends of Manzanar constructed a replica of one of the eight guard towers that ringed the property from 1942 to 1945. The thirty-seven-foot pine tower, guard tower #8, is a reminder of a chapter in

American history that no one wants to remember: not the prisoners, not the military police, not the children who lay in bed at night as the searchlights lit up the barracks. Yet for all those reasons, it was important that the tower be built.

"The tower represents what the whole thing was about: imprisonment, loss of civil liberties, loss of identity," the late Sue Kunitomi Embrey, who was sent to Manzanar when she was nineteen, told the *Los Angeles Times* in 1995. Many of the guards who stood sentry in the towers were from New York and New Jersey and had had little or no exposure to Japanese culture. Military policeman Pat Tortorello, who was stationed at Manzanar with the 322nd Military Police Escort Guard, said no distinction was made between the Japanese American citizens held at the camp and the Japanese combatants whom US soldiers were fighting in Asia. "The Japanese were our enemy and we were there to see that no one escaped," he said. Dennis Tojo, who spent three years at Manzanar as a kid, said the security measures made quite a first impression. "I remember seeing the guard tower and the barbed-wire fence and this blew my mind to think we were going to be behind those wires." In the book

Above left and previous page: Images © Charlie Duncan, Carey & Co. *Above right:* Photograph by Toyo Miyatake, circa 1943, courtesy of Toyo Miyatake Studio.

Children of Manzanar (Heyday, 2012) Annie Sakamoto said she remembered being petrified of the searchlights swooping through the window.

When the war ended in 1945, the internment camp was shut down and the guard towers were torn down. The lumber was sold for scrap. There was some controversy about whether it was a good idea to re-create the watchtower. But in the end, the ideas prevailed. "It's hard for people to admit that we could have built towers to guard our own American citizens," said John Slaughter, who was the National Park Service's facility manager at Manzanar when the tower was built.

BUILT: 1942

AWARDED: 2006

ORIGINAL ARCHITECT: Unknown

SUPERINTENDENT: National Park Service, Tom Leatherman

PRINCIPAL IN CHARGE: Carey & Co. Inc., Alice Carey

PRESERVATION ARCHITECT: Carey & Co. Inc., Charles Duncan

LEAD ENGINEER: DeSimone Consulting Engineers, Mei Liu

The guard tower is visible on the far right in this 1943 photograph by Toyo Miyatake. Image courtesy of Toyo Miyatake Studio.

THE HOME FRONT

The preserved grand houses of California tell the stories of the power-ful capitalists who built much of the state—the railroad magnates, wine barons, and East Coast industrialists who flocked here in the wintertime. And as wonderful as the magnificent mansions are, state preservationists have also fought to save and restore the more modest abodes of the regular people: the factory workers and aspiring actors, the pioneers and dreamers who also shaped the Golden State.

Entry hall of the Beringer Vineyards Rhine House. Image © David Wakely.

GAMBLE HOUSE PASADENA

AFTER SEVEN YEARS OF painstaking preservation work on the Gamble House, architectural historian Edward R. Bosley was a bit taken aback upon hearing his eight-year-old daughter Julia's assessment of the project. "But Papa," she said. "It doesn't look like you did anything to it." That was probably not exactly what Bosley, the Gamble House director, hoped to hear. But after a moment he realized that he had in fact been complimented. "If we had wanted to maintain a light touch on the project, above all doing no harm, and if we had

Above: View of the north exterior at dawn. *Previous page:* Front entry. Both images © Alexander Vertikoff | Vertikoff Archive.

Left: Detail of the front elevation. *Right:* Front patio and door from the northeast corner. Both images © Alexander Vertikoff | Vertikoff Archive.

wanted to allow the rich history of the exterior to continue to be revealed in all of its nicks and scratches, then indeed this was praise to be savored," Bosley recalled in an essay first published in *American Bungalow.*

Designed by architects Greene & Greene, the Gamble House (1907–1909) was commissioned by David and Mary Gamble as a place to escape from Cincinnati's harsh winters. The family (of Procter & Gamble fortune) gave the Greene brothers unusual freedom. In the Gamble House, everything—furniture, built-in cabinetry, leaded stained glass, and landscaping—was the vision of the Greenes. Using teak, mahogany, maple, Port Orford cedar, and oak, the building is a celebration of wood. Its burnished interiors of mahogany and teak, its art-glass windows and obsessive details of crafts-

manship make it a high point of the turn-of-the-century Arts and Crafts style. There may not be another house that so gracefully adheres to William Morris's edict to "blend the useful with the beautiful."

The Gambles lived in the house until their deaths in the 1920s, along with aunt Julia Huggins, who remained there until her death in 1943. Son Cecil Huggins Gamble and his wife took up residence beginning in 1946 and briefly considered selling it, but changed their minds when prospective buyers suggested they might slap a coat of white paint on the interior teak and mahogany. In 1966 the house was given to the City of Pasadena in a joint agreement with the University of Southern California. It has been open to the public ever since.

No matter how lovingly the house was maintained, after more than nine decades it was clear its exterior needed work, said preservation architect Peyton Hall. "If you sit in the California sunshine for a hundred years, it's going to show," he said.

Starting in October 2003 every square inch of the structure was inspected and treated. Rot was removed from rafters, fungus from beam ends, deteriorated varnishes from windows, and failing paint from redwood shakes. The roofing membrane was replaced.

The finishing touch of the exterior project involved the restoration of the one hundred fifty window screens, each of which required twenty hours of rehabilitation. Hall says working on the project was a highlight of his career: "What if you have a resource that is like a work of art that you want to last not for one hundred years—that is way too short a perspective—but one thousand years? What is the level of care and commitment that will keep a fragile resource going for that period of time?"

BUILT: 1909

AWARDED: 2005

ORIGINAL ARCHITECT: Greene & Greene

DIRECTOR: Edward R. Bosley, The Gamble House

PROJECT LEAD: Historic Resources Group, Peyton Hall, FAIA

ARCHITECT: Kelly Sutherlin McLeod Architecture, Inc., Kelly Sutherlin McLeod, AIA

LEAD ENGINEER: Krakower & Associates, Michael Krakower, SE

ARCHITECTURAL CONSERVATOR: Griswold Conservation Associates, John Griswold

GENERAL CONTRACTOR: Voss Industries, George Cavanaugh

East elevation. Image © Alexander Vertikoff | Vertikoff Archive.

CHARLES KRUG WINERY ST. HELENA

AT KRUG WINERY IN St. Helena, the Mondavi family has discovered that vintage stone walls, 1940s redwood tanks, and Civil War–era olive trees are as much a draw as fine cabernets. In 2008 the family, which has owned the winery since 1943, completed an $8 million renovation of two buildings that represent the deepest roots of Napa Valley's oldest commercial winery: an 1861 wine cellar and an 1881 carriage house.

At the grand reopening, Peter Mondavi Jr., a third-generation winemaker, recalled how he used to play hide-and-seek amid the twenty-foot-tall redwood fermentation tanks that created a thicket on the wine cellar floor. He could never have imagined that the wine-soaked redwood from those barrels would one day become the cathedral ceiling rafters and exquisite floors of the winery carriage house. "This was our playground as kids," Mondavi said. "Forty years later, it's still our playground. The redwood tanks as we knew them are gone, but they have returned underfoot and above us."

Prussian immigrant Charles Krug built his wine cellar in 1861. A fire ripped through the structure in 1874, but Krug repaired the damage and continued to expand it and modify it over the years. The room became known as the Redwood Cellar in 1943 when Cesare and Rosa Mondavi purchased the estate for $75,000 and filled it

Above: Redwood Cellar interior after restoration, 2009. *Previous page*: Carriage house exterior after restoration, 2009. Both images © Rien van Rijthoven.

with redwood tanks to ferment their wine. Cesare and Rosa had two sons, Peter and Robert, who had a dramatic falling-out in 1966. While Robert established the famous Robert Mondavi wine business, Peter took over the Charles Krug; in his late nineties now, Peter still lives on the estate, which he runs along with his sons Peter Jr. and Marc. The restoration and seismic-strengthening project, finished in spring of 2008, returned a portion of the Redwood Cellar to its original use, as a barrel-aging room. The carriage house opens onto lush grass where the Mondavis hold "Tastings on the Lawn."

Preservation architect Naomi O. Miroglio of Architectural Resources Group said it is rare that a family-owned business undertakes such a major historical restoration. From a secret Napa quarry, Miroglio's team sourced stone to repair the pink rhyolite used in the

Carriage house interior after restoration, 2009. Image © Rien van Rijthoven.

foundation, in the trim of eighty windows, and in every doorway, arch, and corner of the two buildings. Some 2,257 holes were drilled in the stone walls to accommodate earthquake-reinforcing rods—1,800 in the Redwood Cellar and 457 in the carriage house. "We need to embrace the history—we are an integral part of Napa history, not only Charles Krug but my family as well," said Peter Mondavi Jr.

As it turned out, staves from the redwood fermentation tanks—twenty feet long, eight inches wide, and three inches thick—are good for more than floor planks and rafters. Guitar maker David Heitzman of the Napa Guitar Company thought the wood of the wine-soaked barrels, into which mineral and organic deposits had leached for over half a century, might have an interesting musical tone. "All wood seems to become more musical as time goes by," Heitzman said. He has now made six guitars from the tanks and is auctioning off one a year to raise money for music programs in the Napa schools. At first he made due with the "junk on the bottom" of the tanks because it was what the winery would give him. Now, the Mondavis have embraced the guitar making—and the good publicity it's generating—and Heitzman is happy with what he has. "I don't want the good stuff—I like the idea of the bottom of the barrel," he said. "It makes for a better story."

Detail of carriage house after restoration, 2009. Image © Rien van Rijthoven.

BUILT: 1861 (WINE CELLAR) AND 1881 (CARRIAGE HOUSE)

AWARDED: 2009

OWNER: Charles Krug Winery, The Peter Mondavi Sr. Family

ORIGINAL ARCHITECT: Unknown

ARCHITECT: Architectural Resources Group, Inc., Naomi O. Miroglio

PROJECT LEAD: Degenkolb Engineers, Loring Wyllie Jr.

STRUCTURAL ENGINEER: Degenkolb Engineers, Arne Halterman

GENERAL CONTRACTOR: Andrews & Thornley Construction, Tom Andrews

Carriage house exterior after restoration, 2009. Image © Rien van Rijthoven.

KAUFMANN HOUSE PALM SPRINGS

WHEN BETH AND BRENT Harris bought and restored the Richard Neutra–designed Kaufmann House in Palm Springs, they did more than save a famous house from likely destruction. They catapulted Palm Springs into the spotlight as a vital center of mid-

century modern design. "The Kaufmann house is one of the most iconic houses in the world, and its restoration and all the attention it got really elevated the perception of Palm Springs as a mecca for experimental and interesting modern architecture," said Sidney

Above and opposite: Images © 2013 www.habsphoto.com.

Williams, curator of architecture and design at the Palm Springs Art Museum.

In 1946 Pittsburgh department-store mogul Edgar Kaufmann hired Neutra to design a Palm Springs retreat. With creative freedom and a generous budget—the house cost $350 per square foot, fifty times what an ordinary house cost to build in those days—Neutra went to work on a seminal building that frames the desert's cacti, gray-lavender mountains, and sharp blue sky. The pinwheel-shaped complex features wall-to-wall sliding glass doors that open onto patios. Movable, flexible vertical fins enclose outdoor rooms and offer protection from desert gusts. The architect designed every aspect of the house: the cabinetry, the fixtures that diffuse the overhead light, and the vertical louvers that control sun, shade, and wind. He erected a rooftop gloriette with a hearth, built-in benches, and expansive views. Neutra liked to compare the house to "a ship riding on rocks and sand." He wrote, "Resistance and mutual respect are the basis of friendship between a house and the desert."

Kaufmann died in 1955, and after standing vacant for many years, the house had a series of owners, including Barry Manilow and San Diego Chargers owner Eugene Klein. The various owners remodeled and enlarged the house, enclosed patios, added wallpaper, and removed interior walls. Neutra's original screens of aluminum louvers, blond cabinetry, and many of the original wall surfaces had been removed or radically altered. Floors had been damaged. Douglas fir ceilings had been sandblasted. By the 1990s the house was barely recognizable as the icon that Julius Shulman had so memorably photographed.

Beth and Brent Harris were more architectural tourists than house hunters when in 1993 they reached out to the real-estate broker who was attempting to sell the house. It had been languishing on the market for several years, and the broker indicated clearly to Beth Harris that she felt the land was more valuable than

Above and opposite: Images © 2013 www.habsphoto.com.

the structure on it. The Harrises were horrified. "That was the deciding moment for us," Beth Harris told *CA-Modern* magazine.

After buying the property in 1993 for $1.5 million, the Harrises hired the firm of Marmol Radziner to help with the "forensic restoration." The couple tracked down the original vein of colored stone in a Utah mine for the walls, matched panels of birch veneer for the built-in cabinets, and even bought the machine that was originally used to create the crimped aluminum fascias. They returned counters and floors in bathrooms and kitchens to their original cork. The pool was restored and Marmol Radziner added a pool house that pays homage to Neutra without attempting to mimic his style.

"We weren't looking for a place to live in Palm Springs," Beth Harris said. "We bought the house to restore it. That's the only reason we bought it. To see what it would be like when it was finished. And if we could enjoy it beyond that, that would be the icing on the cake."

BUILT: 1946	ORIGINAL ARCHITECT: Richard Neutra	HISTORIC PRESERVATION CONSULTANT: Seebohm Ltd.
AWARDED: 2000		
	PROJECT LEAD ARCHITECT	LEAD ENGINEER: Cass Rogers, PE
OWNERS: Brent and Beth Harris	CONTRACTOR: Marmol Radziner, Ron Radziner, AIA	

Image © 2013 www.habsphoto.com.

ENNIS HOUSE LOS ANGELES

FRANK LLOYD WRIGHT'S Mayan-style Ennis House in Los Angeles started falling apart before it was even done. Built for entrepreneur Charles Ennis and his wife, Mabel, in 1924, it is the final movement in Wright's quartet of textile block houses—structures assembled from interlocking concrete blocks, inspired by the Mayan buildings in Uxmal. Charles Ennis, the owner of a men's clothing store in downtown L.A., was an enthusiast of Mayan art and architecture.

Convinced that the house should be "of" the hillside rather than on it, Wright integrated the structure into the Los Feliz landscape by using soil from the property to make the concrete blocks. Each of the thirty thousand blocks was handmade using decomposed granite extracted from the site. The patterned blocks, each sixteen inches tall and three and a half inches thick, could be rotated to create different designs on the interior and exterior. Wright said he gravitated to the concrete block because it was "the cheapest (and ugliest) thing in the building world....Why not see what could be done with that gutter rat?"

At Ennis, Wright did a few things with it. He managed to take a cold industrial material and make a dwelling warm and bright. From the dim, low-ceilinged foyer, one ascends up a flight of stairs to a multistory

Above: Dining room with a view of Los Angeles. *Previous page:* View from the great room. Both images © John Vincenti.

living room with russet-colored oak floors and twenty-seven art-glass mosaics, including a famous one of wisteria above the fireplace. The house, overlooking the Los Angeles Basin, was "highly livable," said Janet Tani, whose family owned the property from 1968 to 1980: "One gets to experience the changes of light throughout the day and how that impacts interior spaces on a large scale," she told the *Los Angeles Times*.

But the house had problems from the start. Concrete blocks cracked. Walls buckled under tension. Using decomposed granite from the site turned out to be a bad idea: it introduced natural impurities to the mix, and combined with rusting iron reinforcing bars, caused premature decay. The 1994 earthquake and 2005 record rainfall caused more damage. Later in 2005 the Ennis House Foundation, which by then

Interior hallway. Image © Ron Luxemburg.

owned the property, estimated that stabilization would cost $5 million, and full restoration $15 million. "It is one of the great houses of Los Angeles, and the fact that it was in such poor condition was a big problem," said Linda Dishman, executive director of the Los Angeles Conservancy. "The motor court was literally caving in on itself. There was a retaining wall that was falling apart and crumbling down the hillside after the rains. Everybody worries about earthquakes in California, but the rains can be just as damaging."

Dishman's group joined forces with the Frank Lloyd Wright Building Conservancy and the National Trust for Historic Preservation to buy the house from the foundation that had owned it. With a construction loan and a grant from the Federal Emergency Management Agency, a $6.4 million stabilization and partial resto-ration was completed in 2009. The project included a new structural support system, the restoration or replacement of three thousand damaged blocks, and a new roof. The team also repaired and restored interior woodwork, floors, ceilings, art-glass doors and win-dows, and a mosaic glass-tile mural; painted the kitchen cabinetry its original color; and cleaned interior con-crete blocks.

In 2011 supermarket magnate Ron Burkle bought the house with the intention of finishing the rehabilita-tion. The transition back to private ownership pleased Wright's grandson, Eric Lloyd Wright. "My grandfather designed homes to be occupied by people," he told the *Los Angeles Times*. "His homes are works of art. He cre-ated the space, but the space becomes a creative force and uplifts when it is lived in every day."

Left: Fireplace with mosaic tilework. *Right:* Exterior. Both images © Ron Luxemburg.

BUILT: 1924

AWARDED: 2008

ORIGINAL ARCHITECT:
Frank Lloyd Wright

PROJECT ARCHITECT: Eric Lloyd
Wright & Wiehle-Carr, Associated
Architects; Eric Lloyd Wright, AIA,
and Louis Wiehle, AIA

HISTORIC PRESERVATION
CONSULTANT: Historic Resources
Group, Peyton Hall, FAIA, and
Avigail Charnov

STRUCTURAL ENGINEER:
Melvyn Green and Associates,
Melvyn Green, SE

CONSULTING ENGINEER:
Simpson Gumpertz & Heger,
Inc.; Carolyn Searls, PE, and John
Fidler, RIBA, Associate AIA

GENERAL CONTRACTOR: Matt
Construction, James Muenzer

Ennis House with a view of Los Angeles. Image © Ron Luxemburg.

BERINGER VINEYARDS RHINE HOUSE ST. HELENA

AFTER 124 YEARS, it was hard to believe that Frederick Beringer's Rhine House in St. Helena had any more secrets to reveal. After all, millions of wine tasters had traipsed about the Napa Valley estate. The polished parquet floors were worn down to the nails. The forty-one custom stained-glass windows, including portraits of brothers Frederick and Jacob Beringer, were well documented. Generations of visitors had admired the house's imposing Gothic Victorian exterior and seventeen rooms of handcrafted woodwork. The oldest continually operated vineyard in Napa Valley, the house had been lovingly cared for by the Beringer family, if a bit mucked up by 1970s decor and can lighting fixtures.

Yet one day in 2007, when the winery embarked on a seismic retrofit and renovation of the building, construction workers removed a wooden china case next to the fireplace in the lady's parlor and revealed a swath of burgundy-painted wall. Project architect Naomi O. Miroglio of Architectural Resources Group grabbed a heat gun and peeled away a patch of wallpaper in a corner of the front entrance hall. The beginning of an elaborate hand-painted banner was uncovered. It said *Willkommen*—German for "Welcome."

"We felt like we had a message from the past—Frederick was speaking to us," said Miroglio.

Five more green-and-burgundy teardrop-shaped banners were uncovered in all, though some were in bad condition, with missing letters. A German professor

Above left: Outdoor seating area.. *Above right*: Restored tasting room with new wine-tasting bar. *Opposite*: Exterior. All images © David Wakely.

agreed to "exchange words for wine" and see if he could decipher the hand-stenciled message on the banners. He quickly cracked the code, determining that it was a quote from a common German national song. The translation was: "Welcome, who with heart and hand will ever in friendship meet." Miroglio said it still gives her the chills. "Have you ever seen a message like that in decoration before?" she asked.

In a way, the Rhine House, completed in 1884 by architect Albert Schroepfer, has always been about conveying a statement. In a part of the country where the wine business was still in its infancy, the house's opulence sent the message that European winemakers could find success in the New World. Legend has it that Frederick Beringer wanted to recreate a Rhine Valley villa from his childhood in Mainz on the Rhine, but there is no concrete evidence that the design was inspired by any particular home back in Germany. Built at a cost of about $28,000 (with the forty-one panels of stained glass accounting for $6,000) the gabled Rhine House is a classic example of ornate Victorian architecture.

Gift shop. Image © David Wakely.

In addition to seismic upgrades required by the City of St. Helena, the project included several phases of restoration: the conservation of the stained-glass windows, the restoration of the floors, and the installation of a geothermal heating and cooling system deep beneath the spacious front lawn to neutralize heat loss in the building in the winter and optimize cooling in the summer. "It was a spectacularly well-built structure—the tradition for the stonemasons in Napa Valley was profound and the quality of stonework on these is just incredible," said Miroglio. "We did very little repair."

BUILT: 1884

AWARDED: 2009

ORIGINAL ARCHITECT:
Albert Schroepfer

PROJECT LEAD: Foster's Wine Estates Americas, Doug Roberts

ARCHITECTURE, PLANNING, AND CONSERVATION: Architectural Resources Group, Inc., Naomi O. Miroglio

STRUCTURAL ENGINEER: Abey Structural, Keith Abey

GLASS CONSERVATION:
Nzilani Glass Conservation, Ariana Makau

GENERAL CONTRACTOR:
Bruce Tucker Construction, Inc., Scot Johnson

Restored stencil panels. Image © David Wakely.

CASE STUDY HOUSE #18 LOS ANGELES

WHEN THE NORTHRIDGE earthquake struck on the moonless night of January 17, 1994, Fran Nathanson woke up in a tangle of plaster, glass, and blood. Her Pacific Palisades house seemed to have caved in around her. Soffits had collapsed, glass walls had shattered. The seventy-year-old Nathanson had a gash across her forehead. She wanted to get up; her husband Leo held her tight. "It's a good thing he didn't let me get up because there was glass all over the floor, which I couldn't see

at 4:00 a.m.," said Nathanson, who later received eighteen stitches.

The next day the Nathansons, like homeowners all over L.A., surveyed the wreckage. Their U-shaped midcentury modern house hadn't fared well. The floor-to-ceiling brick fireplace had collapsed, leaving a heap of bricks on the floor. The foundation had sunk into the fill the house was built on, twisting the exterior walls apart.

Top: The unreinforced masonry fireplace collapsed during the Northridge earthquake. *Bottom:* The fireplace was restored with salvaged brick from the original structure. *Opposite:* Restored Pacific Ocean facade. All images © Gordon A. Olschlager, AIA.

But unlike other Angelenos, the Nathansons had some powerful allies as they set about rebuilding their residence. They didn't just live in any old house: they lived in a Case Study house. The Case Study Houses program was a post–World War II experiment in home building sponsored by *Arts & Architecture* magazine. In January 1945, as returning veterans fueled an unprecedented housing boom, magazine editor John Entenza had an idea. He knew technological breakthroughs during the war would forever change residential construction. He challenged designers to construct efficient and inexpensive homes "using war-born techniques and materials best-suited to the expression of man's life in the Modern world." He reached out to major architects of the day—Richard Neutra, Charles and Ray Eames, and Eero Saarinen—and commissioned them to build houses that would be featured in the magazine and open to the public. The first six houses were built by 1948 and attracted more than 350,000 visitors.

The Rodney Walker–designed Nathanson house is Case Study House #18. The oceanfront structure, perched over Pacific Coast Highway, was built almost entirely out of mass-produced plywood, the interior boards covered with a walnut veneer. The building

Restored living room. Image © Gordon A. Olschlager, AIA.

had an open floor plan, unusual for the time, and sliding glass walls connecting indoors and outdoors. The house is small—1,200 square feet—but built-in cabinets, bookshelves, and storage make it feel bigger.

After the earthquake, it wasn't long before the Los Angeles preservation community reached out to see how the house had held up. Architect Gordon A. Olschlager wrote an assessment of the damage. "Los Angeles Conservancy offered to help us financially as long as we used as much of the [original] materials as we could," Olschlager said.

New foundations were built under the entire house, but the wood was salvaged. The new fireplace was made out of reinforced concrete with the original bricks saved for the face. The original Pullman kitchen was left intact. A small addition connected the house and adjacent garage. "We tried to minimize how much the addition engaged the original house," Olschlager said. "The addition was designed to be reversible. If someone was a purist and wanted to take it out, they could and the original facade is still there."

Nathanson, now eighty-seven, paid $115,000 for the house in 1975. She knew nothing about the Case Study Houses project at the time. "It's been wonderful to be part of," she said. "I think the house was very well designed."

BUILT: 1948

AWARDED: 1996

OWNER: Leo and Frances Nathanson

ORIGINAL ARCHITECT: Rodney Walker

ARCHITECT: John Ash Group Architects, Gordon A. Oschlager, AIA

ENGINEER: Wheeler & Gray, Inc., Les Schulz, PE

Restored Pacific Ocean facade. Image © Gordon A. Olschlager, AIA.

LELAND STANFORD MANSION SACRAMENTO

CHARLOTTE M. SHULTZ, a San Francisco social-ite, remembers arriving at the capitol in Sacramento in 2005 to report to duty after Governor Arnold Schwar-zenegger had appointed her chief of protocol. "I got there and said, 'Where is my office?' They said there was no office. I said, 'Where is my staff?' They said there was no staff. I said, 'Where is the money?' They said there was no money." Schultz walked to the nearby Stanford Mansion, which was undergoing a $22 mil-lion, fourteen-year restoration. "I said, 'Let's finish this thing because we need someplace to entertain heads of state,'" she recalled.

The Leland Stanford Mansion State Historic Park is forty-four rooms of Victorian splendor hemmed in by a dreary block of bureaucratic midrise towers. Originally built by a gold-rush merchant, the house is a testimony to the ambitions of Leland Stanford: railroad magnate, governor, US senator, and cofounder of Stanford University. In June of 1861, Stanford, then the Republican candidate for governor, bought the property for $8,000, thinking it would be an appropriate abode for the Golden State's top elected official. Stanford served as governor for one two-year term. Two subsequent governors, Frederick Low and Henry Haight, also used the mansion as their seat of power.

In 1871 Stanford returned to the house and embarked on a vast expansion propelled by his newfound wealth as one of the "Big Four" barons of the transcontinental railroad. The original two-story house was jacked up so that a new first floor could be slid underneath. A fourth floor was added with a mansard roof, reflecting the trendy French Second Empire design favored in the day. The new house grew from four thousand to nineteen thousand square feet. In February of 1872 seven

Above left: Rear vehicular courtyard prior to restoration, showing an enclosed porch, an exterior fire-escape route, and nonhistoric enclosures over the porch. *Above right:* The back courtyard after restoration. Images courtesy of Page & Turnbull. *Opposite:* Image © California State Parks, Leland Stanford Mansion State Historic Park.

hundred guests celebrated the reopening of what the newspaper *The California Farmer* succinctly pronounced "the most perfect specimen of a residence in this state."

After just two years in the newly renovated house, the Stanfords decamped to San Francisco's Nob Hill, where they constructed an even more opulent mansion. The old house in rapidly developing Sacramento stood empty for twenty-six years. In 1900, Leland's wife, Jane Stanford, gave the mansion to the Catholic Diocese of Sacramento, with an endowment of $75,000 "for the nurture, care and maintenance of homeless children." Surprisingly, the mansion and its furniture survived the decades of children relatively intact. The children were moved to a more modern facility in the 1970s when the State of California acquired the mansion to be used as a state park. In 1991 Governor Pete Wilson's wife, Gayle Wilson, kicked off an effort to raise money to restore the mansion and make it into a museum and ceremonial venue.

Photographs commissioned in Stanford's day helped guide the interior restoration. Much of the missing

Above: Restored Gentleman's Parlor, 2005. *Opposite:* Fully restored facade, 2005. Both images © Gino Creglia.

original Renaissance Revival furniture was hunted down or replicated. Lace draperies and opulent carpets were re-created, as were glass panels in the mansion's grand front doors. Carpenters restored the bedroom in which Jane Stanford gave birth to the couple's only child, Leland Jr., the namesake of Stanford University. A web of white netting stretches in a canopy above the carved child-sized bed. Leland Jr.'s toys are there: ice skates, roller skates, riding clothes and tack, barbells, and two pairs of leather boxing gloves. In contrast are the toys left behind by the Stanford Home for Children: clay marbles and jacks, a rusted fire wagon, and broken porcelain doll heads.

Once the restoration of the mansion was complete, Governor Schwarzenegger entertained Mexico's President Vicente Fox, the Czech Republic's President Václav Klaus, and many other heads of state there. "The house was almost like a good ghost," said Schultz. "I would get goose bumps thinking about all the things that happened there."

BUILT: 1861, 1872

AWARDED: 2006

OWNER: California Department of Parks and Recreation

ORIGINAL ARCHITECT: Seth Babson

ARCHITECT: Maria Baranowski, AIA, California Department of Parks and Recreation

LANDSCAPE ARCHITECT: PGA Design

GENERAL CONTRACTOR: Reyman Brothers Construction

ARCHEOLOGIST: Dick Hastings, California Department of Parks and Recreation

Image © California State Parks, Leland Stanford Mansion State Historic Park.

HOLLYWOOD BUNGALOW COURTS LOS ANGELES

THE HOLLYWOOD Community Housing Corporation is on a mission to save a classic but often-threatened Los Angeles housing type: the bungalow court. Twice the affordable-housing developer has intervened to protect Hollywood bungalow courts facing the wrecking ball. The first time, in 1995, the city wanted the sixteen-unit St. Andrews Bungalow Court knocked down after drug dealers had turned it into a haven for addicts. HCHC stepped in and renovated the sixteen units, leasing them at below-market rents to disabled Angelenos with HIV/AIDS. "The

buildings were burned down, run-down, and uninhabited. They were a blight," said Bill Harris, who heads up HCHC.

Fast-forward to 2009, and the Hollywood Bungalow Courts, four properties clustered on Serrano Avenue and Kingsley Drive, were facing a double threat of neglect and rising land values. The properties were unkempt and crime-ridden but were also attracting the interest of infill-housing developers who saw a chance to cash in with higher densities in an improving neighborhood. The property owners had moved to Paris, and

Above left: View of typical built-in cabinetry. *Above right:* Kitchen. *Previous page:* A typical interior. All images courtesy of M2A Milofsky, Michali and Cox Architects.

wanted out. Again, HCHC revived the historic properties and leased them out to disabled adults, many of whom had previously been homeless.

In restoring Hollywood's bungalow courts, HCHC accomplished more than just housing needy populations. It preserved an endangered category of building that embodies the sunny optimism and opportunities of early Hollywood. From 1915 to the late 1920s the bungalow court was the perfect architectural response to Hollywood's burgeoning entertainment industry. In the 1920s the population of Hollywood grew from 35,000 to 115,000. In a bungalow courtyard, an aspiring actor, writer, or set designer might find the perfect combination of affordable independence and Southern Californian egalitarianism. The bungalows, Colonial Revival and Spanish Revival, were separate dwellings but shared common courtyards and parking. Many had built-in features—bookshelves, ironing boards, Murphy beds, breakfast tables, dressers—perfect for the Hollywood newcomer showing up with little more than a suitcase. "There is a sense of nostalgia—they hearken back to a simpler, more innocent time," said Harris.

HCHC saved much of the original windows, woodwork, and landscaping—camellias, boxwoods, and fruit trees. But much work had to be done. The bungalows had termite and dry-rot issues; tar paper had allowed water to leak in, which created mold. Several of the bungalows were taken down to the studs on the exterior due to severe stucco deterioration, and were then given new waterproofing. "The designers [HCHC] have a real flair for less is more," said Christy McAvoy of Historic Resources Group, the preservation consultant on the project. "These are simple cottages. HCHC did not gussy them up. They just fixed them. Anyone would be extremely comfortable there."

When Jim Dunn moved into St. Andrews Bungalow Court fifteen years ago, he had been evicted and was sleeping on friends' couches. "I was over the moon," said Dunn. "It's heaven. In a regular apartment building I don't know what I would do. I don't know if I could handle the closeness."

There are not too many bungalow courts left. Pasadena has some, as do Santa Barbara and a few other places. Today's large apartment complexes are all about efficiency, with one boiler and HVAC system serving dozens of units. Bungalows, with their independent systems, would cost a fortune. "You can't build these anymore," said Harris.

BUILT: 1920S

AWARDED: 2010

OWNER: Hollywood Community Housing Corporation, William Harris

ORIGINAL ARCHITECT: Unknown

PROJECT ARCHITECT: M2A Milofsky, Michali and Cox Architects, Tom Michali and Nina Avanessian

HISTORIC CONSULTANT: Historic Resource Group, Christy McAvoy

STRUCTURAL ENGINEER: Structural Focus, Wayne Chang

GENERAL CONTRACTOR: Dreyfuss Construction, Jim Dreyfuss

View of the north side of the courtyard. Image courtesy of M2A Milofsky, Michali and Cox Architects.

WARNER BARN AND RANCH HOUSE SAN DIEGO

THE PLACE FAMOUS AS Warner's Ranch was never really Warner's Ranch. But that doesn't make it any less important.

For decades historians of western migration relied on old maps, folklore, and circumstantial evidence to identify the house and trading post of Juan José Warner, an American-born ranchero aristocrat and land grantee who ran a trading post in high desert country east of San Diego. It was conventional wisdom that the 1857 adobe brick house and 1844 hand-hewn barn overlooking the Arroyo de Buena Vista had been the property of Warner.

But as architectural historians started in on the restoration of the property in 2005, questions arose about the accuracy of the story. Warner's ranch had been burned during an 1851 Indian uprising, according to multiple accounts. Yet how come there were no charred remains on the site? Later, archeologists found that in actuality, Warner's house had been located nearby on the north side of Arroyo de Buena Vista.

Research now suggests that, in fact, the adobe known as Warner's Ranch was the home of Doña Vicenta Sepúlveda de Carrillo, a prominent female rancher. The ranch served the Butterfield Stage Stop from

Above left and right: Barn interior after stabilization, 2012. *Opposite:* Northwest elevation of the barn after stabilization, 2012. All images © larnymack.com.

1858 until the beginning of the Civil War in 1861. For emigrants traveling to the California settlements and goldfields, the barn was the first well-supplied trading post reached after traversing the Santa Fe Trail. After "thinking they had made the biggest mistake of their life, that they had been sold a bill of goods," the settlers would get up into the high desert country and find forage for their oxen and a place to rest at the ranch, said Bruce Coons, the executive director of Save Our Heritage Organization, which is converting the house and barn into a museum.

"It's the only place in California where you can experience those dramatic views the pioneers saw as they crossed the great southwest desert," said Coons. "It was the first well-watered valley they saw—they were over-joyed and thought...there is a promised land after all, and we didn't do this for nothing."

It was the fork in the road of all forks in the road. To the right were the goldfields, to the left the road to San Diego. In 1858 Waterman Ormsby, correspondent for the *New York Herald,* described the way station as a "comfortable house situated in the valley, in the midst of a beautiful meadow, and its shingled roof looked more like civilization than anything I had seen for many days."

Until the 1960s the Warner-Carrillo Ranch House remained a boarding place for cowboys who worked for George Sawday. Career cowboys such as Zeb and Gib Reed stayed there while noted celebrities dropped by, captivated by the culture of the fading Wild West. Will

Rogers visited in the 1930s. John Wayne exchanged cowboy hats with Sawday at the ranch in the 1940s, and later wore the hat in question in the Western film *She Wore a Yellow Ribbon.*

In 1946 the Vista Irrigation District took ownership of the land. The ranch sat vacant and mostly ignored for decades until 2000, when the Save Our Heritage Organization put it on their most-endangered-building list. Even then, the Vista Irrigation District resisted any notion that it might help preserve the property.

That changed when Roy Coox, a college history major, became the general manager of the water district. Coox was enchanted by the history but found the ranch house in terrible shape: full of bats, the adobe walls crumbling, the canvas canopy draped below the ceiling in tatters. He secured public and private funds for the barn and house restoration, while minimizing the amount of district money spent on it. So far, the farmhouse has been fully restored, while the barn has been stabilized. "We took it as far as the money would go," said Coox.

BUILT: 1849

AWARDED: 2009

OWNER: Vista Irrigation District, Roy Coox

ORIGINAL ARCHITECT: Unknown

PROJECT LEAD AND HISTORIC ARCHITECT: IS Architecture, Ione Stiegler, AIA

STRUCTURAL ENGINEER: Melvyn Green and Associates, Melvyn Green, SE

GENERAL CONTRACTOR: Mark Sauer Construction, Inc., Mark Sauer

Detail of barn roof after stabilization, 2012. Image © larnymack.com.

SIKES ADOBE FARMHOUSE ESCONDIDO

RAISING MONEY TO RESTORE a nineteenth-century farmhouse in backcountry San Diego is hard enough to do once. At the Sikes Adobe Farmhouse in Escondido, preservationists had to do it twice. The 1870-era adobe brick farmhouse had just been restored when the 2007 Witch Creek wildfire, the second worst wildfire in Southern California history, engulfed it and one thousand residential buildings between the Santa Ysabel canyon and Rancho Santa Fe. "It was pretty heart wrenching—so much love, so much effort had

gone into that original restoration, and it was hard to picture at the time that we would be able to come back from it," said project architect Ione Stiegler.

Before its destruction, the humble farmhouse offered a rare glimpse into the lives of pioneers who arrived in San Diego in the 1800s. It told the story of Zenas and Eliza Sikes, who in 1868 uprooted the family from the Bay Area and built a one-room adobe brick house on 2,400 acres of what was then Rancho San Bernardo. Before long, the growing family of eight needed more

space, and built wood additions and porches. The family farmed wheat for several years before turning the homestead into a dairy farm. Zenas was a community leader and the first postmaster of San Bernardo.

Along with the farmhouse, which had remained in good shape until its first restoration in 2004, Eliza Sikes left behind valuable, meticulous records of her daily life. After Zenas Sikes died in 1881—he was kicked twice in the same leg by an ornery mule and died on the operating table—his widow was required to keep extensive records for probate court: correspondence, receipts, shopping lists. The records suggest that after her husband died, Eliza Sikes entered into what Stiegler calls her "merry widow period." She collected $6,000 in life insurance and was not afraid to spend it. Her most extravagant acquisition was a $600 Steinway Piano—equal to about $14,000 today. Her other passion seems to have been interior decoration. She moved the front door and added bedrooms and a wraparound veranda.

The records also indicate that Eliza Sikes bought a lot of wallpaper—six major purchases in nine years. Yet none of the preservationists could figure out what she had done with it—until one day Stiegler removed some rotted wood. "Lo and behold, behind the wood were seven layers of wallpaper," she recalled. "The floral patterns were more and more robust as you headed into the Victorian era."

Above: The sitting room was wallpapered to match the pattern chosen by Eliza Sykes in 1881. Image © 2012 larnymack.com. *Previous two pages:* Image © 2012 larnymack.com.

After the fire it didn't take long for the same crew that had done the first restoration to get to work rebuilding the farmhouse. Using the remaining adobe walls and the original floor plans as guides, the team built an exact replica of the original. The work was funded by the insurance company and the Washington, DC–based Federal Emergency Management Agency (FEMA)—though "some on the FEMA staff questioned the allocation, saying, 'Back east this is just a pile of mud. How do I justify spending these tax dollars on a mud hut?'" said Anne Cooper, who manages the Sikes Adobe Farmhouse. "I told him that for us, this is important. This is our early agricultural history. We don't have a 'George Washington slept here.'"

BUILT: 1872

AWARDED: 2003, 2005, and 2011

OWNER: San Dieguito River Park, Susan Carter, Deputy Director

ORIGINAL ARCHITECT: Unknown

PRESERVATION ARCHITECT: IS Architecture, Ione Stiegler, AIA, LEED AP, Michael Martinez, AIA

LEAD ENGINEER: Melvyn Green and Associates, Melvyn Green, SE, and Anja Kluge, PE

LANDSCAPE ARCHITECT: Wallace, Roberts & Todd, Laura Burnett Wallace

CULTURAL RESOURCE CONSULTANT: Vonn Marie May

GENERAL CONTRACTOR: Mark Sauer Construction, Inc., Mark Sauer

HISTORIAN: Walter Enterprises, Stephen Van Wormer

Restored kitchen, 2012. Image © 2012 larnymack.com.

HERCULES WORKMEN'S COTTAGES HERCULES

STEVE LAWTON FIRST NOTICED the postindustrial remnants of the Hercules Powder Company in the 1970s, when he was a brakeman on the Southern Pacific Railroad. From the cab of his locomotive he watched the East Bay's industrial ghost towns slip by: the defunct low-slung factory buildings, the unidentifiable rusty equipment. Scattered here and there amid open fields were vacant white, wooden workers' cottages. "It was a weed-covered site with crumbling, dilapidated houses," said Lawton. Lawton didn't know it at the time, but the historic company town of Hercu-

les was destined not only to become his home but also a place that he would spend decades researching and fighting to protect.

Hercules was the largest of the East Bay's company towns, which included Giant (Giant Powder), Oleum (Union Oil), and Selby (American Smelting and Refining). Of them all, Hercules is also the only town in which a significant portion of the company housing now remains intact. The town emerged as an industrial center in 1879 when the California Powder Works bought a tract of land on San Pablo Bay. The

Above left: Queen Anne cottage after restoration. *Above right:* Restored interior. *Previous page:* Colonial Revival homes after restoration. All images courtesy of Architectural Resources Group.

company, which manufactured explosives, had previously operated in Santa Cruz and San Francisco but wanted to relocate far away from people and neighborhoods, which would be blown to smithereens during inevitable mishaps. (The concerns were well founded: during the first forty years of operations at Hercules, fifty-nine workers died in explosions.) Hercules was the world's leading producer of TNT during World War I, and for seventy-five years remained a company town with fewer than three hundred residents, according to a book on the town Lawton wrote with Jennifer Posedel.

Eventually, the company started building housing for its workers. Chinese workers, who made up the bulk of the Hercules workforce in the nineteenth century, lived in wooden dormitories on the waterfront. In the late 1890s a stately home called White Columns was built on the hill above the plant for the superintendent, in addition to a dozen cottages for middle managers. The village eventually grew to some one hundred houses and duplexes. During World War I, additional lodging—homes, dorms, and a residential hotel—were erected to shelter the growing workforce.

By the late 1970s the plant—which had been converted to a fertilizer plant in 1964—was shuttered, and the homes had been razed or become dilapidated. In the early 1980s the city conducted a historical architectural survey and found that twenty homes were in good enough shape to save—three stylish Queen Anne homes and seventeen simpler Colonial Revivals. The town of Hercules picked developer Peter Supino and preservation architect Architectural Resources Group to formulate a blueprint. Supino reconstructed the original town plan, built new streets and sidewalks, and moved thirteen of the twenty buildings into a cohesive group. "The context needed to be strengthened—in some cases there was a streetscape and no houses, and in some cases there were houses and no streetscape," said Stephen Farneth of Architectural Resources Group. "It needed to feel like an old-fashioned neighborhood."

The houses were rented out for five years and sold in 1989. One of the first buyers was Lawton, the former South Pacific brakeman, who had been living in West Berkeley. "We were looking for a vintage house," said Lawton. "These had character. It was a little haven of new urbanism out by the bay."

The buildings tell the story of the first example of industrial innovation in the West, said Lawton. "What we are known for in California, and especially the Bay Area, is taking science and inventing new processes and new products that create industries. This is the first time that occurred."

BUILT: LATE 1890S

AWARDED: 1986

DEVELOPER: Peter Supino

ORIGINAL ARCHITECT: Unknown

PRESERVATION ARCHITECT: Architectural Resources Group, Stephen Farneth AIA

Colonial Revival homes before restoration. Image courtesy of Architectural Resources Group.

CREATIVE REUSE

Vacant landmark buildings keep preservationists up at night. Fires and earthquakes threaten. Developers and investors hover. City officials and neighbors lose patience with blighted structures. Funds for restoration are scarce, and the requirements of historic rehabilitation can be onerous for potential tenants. But every once in a while everything lines up: the perfect use, the ideal user, and the money to do the work. And fresh life is breathed into a grand but long-suffering structure.

Craneway Pavilion interior, Ford Assembly Building, 2008. Image © Billy Hustace Photography.

AFRICAN AMERICAN MUSEUM AND LIBRARY
OAKLAND

IN 1989 AND 1990 the Italian Renaissance library on Fourteenth Street in downtown Oakland suffered what seemed like a one-two knockout. First, in October the Loma Prieta earthquake struck, shaking loose much of the building's unreinforced masonry and ornate plaster ceilings. Next, looters broke in and made off with some of the original oak balustrades. "From the time when we originally surveyed the damage to when we went back for the renovation, a lot of the oak was gone," said project architect Michael Willis.

· SHAKESPEARE ·

FREE TO ALL

AFRICAN AMERICAN
MUSEUM & LIBRARY
OAKLAND

AMERICAN MUSEUM &

AMERICAN MUSEUM LIBRARY

Above: Main stair hallway with administration/archive/museum store area through the glass wall and doors. Image © George Celli, African American Museum & Library, Oakland. *Opposite:* Image © 2012 Matthew Roth/Wikimedia Commons/CC-BY-SA-3.0. *Previous page:* Image © George Celli, African American Museum & Library, Oakland.

The 1902 Beaux-Arts building, designed by Bliss & Faville, was the first of five libraries in Oakland funded by industrialist Andrew Carnegie. (All together Carnegie provided grants for 142 California libraries; 82 still stand.) From the start, the symmetrical building was a testament to Oakland's high-minded library program. A mix of brick, stone, and terra-cotta, its exterior was ringed with the names of classical scholars engraved in stone. Inside, tall, recessed, arched windows illuminated oak paneling and stairways, coffered and stenciled plaster ceilings, and murals by early-twentieth-century painters Arthur Mathews and Marion Holden. Lest library patrons forget the seriousness of literary

endeavors, the ceiling of the reading room was adorned with the names of the writers from the Western canon, from Thackeray to Longfellow to Shakespeare.

But all of that was in danger in the aftermath of the earthquake. The Oakland Heritage Alliance fought for the building's preservation, but it was not clear if any organization was interested in occupying it. Finally, the African American Museum and Library at Oakland emerged as a perfect tenant, and $11.5 million was raised from federal, state, and local sources.

The building's old frame was dismantled and then put together again after a new concrete frame and steel roof members had been installed. Enough of the original wood and plaster details survived that the construction team was able to make molds from existing plaster forms and to recreate the wood detail in the workshop. Other details were pieced together from photographs. The oak staircase and paneling, murals, and classical columns all were restored or rebuilt. "There were woodworkers who delayed their retirement to finish this project," said Willis.

The new museum and library opened on February 24, 2002, with African American writers and scholars like Maya Angelou and Lani Guinier in attendance. AAMLO today is a treasure trove of information about African American history on the West Coast and beyond. It has a twelve-thousand-volume library, and a microfilm collection that includes primary research information on African American enslavement and

New and refurbished oak millwork. Image © George Celli, African American Museum & Library, Oakland.

military service, and on Marcus Garvey's Universal Negro Improvement Association, as well as California census records from 1910 through 1930.

During the renovation there was a push to replace the all-white writers' names memorialized in the reading room with the names of writers of color. Willis, African American himself, fought to keep the building's historic integrity. "We don't have to say that Shakespeare didn't exist in order to say that James Baldwin did," he explained.

BUILT: 1902

AWARDED: 2003

OWNER: City of Oakland, Public Works Agency

ORIGINAL ARCHITECT: Bliss & Faville

ARCHITECT: Michael Willis Architects, Jeffrey J. McGraw

LEAD ENGINEER: Rutherford & Chekene

STRUCTURAL ENGINEER: GSC Associates

GENERAL CONTRACTOR: Lindquist-Van Hook, Mark Lindquist

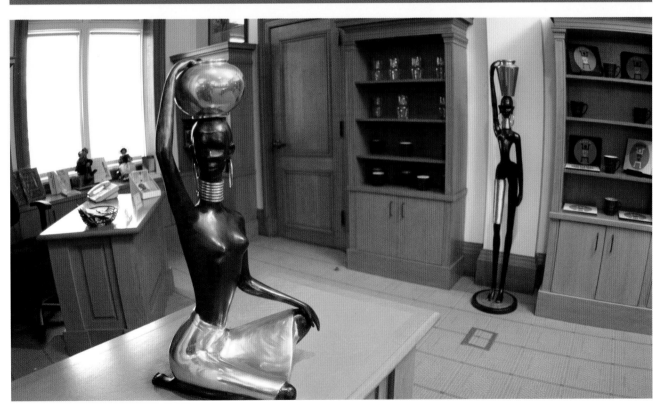

Image © George Celli, African American Museum & Library, Oakland.

MARY ANDREWS CLARK MEMORIAL HOME
LOS ANGELES

RENÉ CASTRO HAD FALLEN on hard times and lost his house to the bank when in 1996 he landed, through a lottery, an affordable room at the Mary Edwards Clark Memorial Home. Although Castro grew up in Los Angeles, he was unprepared for what he found when he arrived. "It's a huge castle—not something you see every day in Los Angeles," said Castro, seventy-five and a retired cook for the Los Angeles Unified School District. Now Castro spends his days playing flamenco guitar and composing love songs in the single-occupancy room with sweeping views of the downtown Los Angeles skyline. Castro is one of 152 residents bringing new purpose to one of Los Angeles's most unusual landmarks.

The Mary Andrews Clark Home is a French Colonial brick chateau in the Westlake neighborhood. William A. Clark, a copper magnate, built the house in 1913 as a "perpetual memorial" to his mother, Mary Andrews Clark, who died in Los Angeles. At a time when young single women were streaming into L.A., Clark dreamed of creating a home the newcomers could "live in delight and comfort at a price which every woman can afford."

It would be a safe, cultured environment where women could find community.

Clark handed the architecture responsibilities over to Arthur Burnett Benton. Benton designed a U-shaped brick mansion punctuated with gables, cupolas, turrets, and balconies. The first floor held the lobby, the administration offices, a large reception hall, two private parlors, a dining-room library, a three-hundred-seat lecture room, and a gymnasium. The rest of the building held dormitories for two hundred girls, as well as sleeping porches, sewing- and workrooms, classrooms, a laundry, and a complete hospital suite.

Above: Library with restored woodwork, 1994. *Opposite:* Second-floor porch looking into the lounge, 1994. Both images © J. Scott Photography.

For $5.05 a week, tenants got a room, two daily meals, and use of the sewing machines and laundry. There were book clubs, dancing parties, bowling nights, and tennis tournaments. At the time it opened, the group of residents included sixty-six stenographers, twenty-eight instructors, twenty-seven office helpers, twenty saleswomen, ten dressmakers, six nurses, five artists, five manicurists, four milliners, and two librarians. Rules were strict: residents could not drink alcohol, entertain male friends upstairs, or wear curlers at dinner. The property's "immaculately kept lawns, wide verandas and inviting lawn-tennis court seem more in line with the advantages that are usually associated with the residence of a family of wealth and position than the home of girls who find it necessary to work for a living," the *Los Angeles Times* wrote in 1926.

The YWCA operated the house from 1913 to 1987, when it was closed down after the Whittier Narrows earthquake rendered it unsafe. In 1990 the YWCA sold the building for $3 million to the Los Angeles Community Design Center, a nonprofit group. Crews were putting the finishing touches on the building's seismic upgrade and renovation when the Northridge earthquake struck in 1994, crumbling a fifth-floor balcony. Had the reinforcement not been completed, the building would probably have been lost.

Above left: Stair shaft and linoleum floor, 1994. *Above right:* Second-floor lounge's repaired marble fireplace, which was hand sculpted in Scotland and cracked during the 1987 Whittier Narrows earthquake, 1994. Both images © J. Scott Photography.

South elevation of the north wing showing one of the original Queen Palm trees, 1994. Image © J. Scott Photography.

Led by preservationist Christy McAvoy of Historic Resources Group, the new owner renovated the building and reopened it in 1995 as housing for single workers making less than $17,650 per year. Tom Polaski, director of facility management for the house, said the building—with its oak windows, glazed brick, copper gutters, and stained-glass library windows—could never be replicated; "We could never afford to build something like this from scratch." The home's architectural solidity adds to the security and stabilization of the residents, many of whom have had difficult lives. "It's an island of peacefulness on a gritty corner," said Polaski.

BUILT: 1913

AWARDED: 1995

OWNER: Crescent Bay Company; Los Angeles Community Design Center

ORIGINAL ARCHITECT: Arthur Burnett Benton

ARCHITECT: Killefer Flammang Purtill Architects, Frank Purtill, AIA, Principal-in-Charge

PRESERVATION ARCHITECT: Historic Resources Group, Christy McAvoy

CONTRACTORS: W. E. O'Neil Construction Company

Stained-glass windows in the library, 1994. Image © J. Scott Photography.

FERRY BUILDING SAN FRANCISCO

THE GEARS AND PENDULUMS of the nine-hundred-pound Ferry Building clock had been cleaned of a century of soot when, at noon on Tuesday, June 17 of 2003, Mayor Willie Brown ceremoniously revived San Francisco's most famous timepiece. "The restart-ing of the clock signals the Ferry Building's return to public service as an icon on the vibrant waterfront," said Mayor Brown. For once, a politician's proclama-tion turned out to be understated.

Since reopening, the Ferry Building has become the civic gathering place the city didn't know it needed. It is a physical manifestation of Northern California's

Above left: During restoration. *Above right:* View of the clock tower after restoration. Both images © Tom Paiva Photography. *Opposite and previous page:* Image © Richard Barnes/OTTO.

position on the forefront of a movement that celebrates local, organic produce and meats. Six million people visit the building each year.

The Beaux-Arts transit hall was designed by A. Page Brown and completed in 1898. When it opened, the building's interior was dominated by the Great Nave, a 660-foot-long, sky-lit, two-story concourse on the second floor that provided access to the ferries. The Nave was a cathedral of steel arched trusses, brick and terra-cotta ornament, crossed lattice windows, and Tennessee marble walls. The floor was nearly as spectacular:

a decorative marble mosaic with a large rendering of the Great Seal of the State of California. And then there was the 245-foot clock tower, modeled after the Giralda Cathedral in Seville, Spain.

By the 1950s the building suffered from two decisions that would take fifty years to reverse. In 1954 the Great Nave was cut in half when a floor and mezzanines were inserted to create office space for the Port of San Francisco. And the desire to move automobile traffic efficiently through the city prompted erection of an elevated freeway directly in front of the building.

Once a grand exclamation point at the foot of Market Street, suddenly the clock tower was a relic that peeked furtively above the snarl of traffic.

The 1989 Loma Prieta earthquake badly damaged the elevated freeway, prompting city officials to tear it down altogether. When it was cleared away, a group of organic farmers proposed a market where the freeway once stood. The idea took off. "It was brilliant because it was establishing the public realm in the Embarcadero in a way that was really amazing," said project architect Cathy Simon of Perkins & Will (then SMWM).

Meanwhile, the Port of San Francisco relocated its offices to a rehabilitated Pier 1 structure and solicited proposals from developers interested in rehabilitating the old Ferry Building. While other competing developers proposed more conventional retail, a team led by developer Wilson Meany Sullivan and SMWM envisioned a locally sourced, European-style food market with no designated parking. "Everyone said it would never work, that nobody would go there because how can you shop without parking?" recalled Simon.

The developer and design team traveled to Europe to study markets in Paris, London, and Venice. They saw how the best markets open up and spill out into the streets, how produce is displayed on wheeled carts that can be rolled in and out. Back in San Francisco they got to work, finalizing a plan to convert the ground-floor baggage area into a sixty-five-thousand-square-foot public food market. There were tough decisions as well. The developer wanted to cut two large openings in the floor of the nave, so that the soaring steel roof trusses and skylights would be visible from the ground-floor food market. But that required cutting holes into the mosaic flooring on the concourse level, an important part of the building's historic character. In the end, the developers received permission to do it, but not without intervention by US Representative Nancy Pelosi and an emergency trip to Washington, DC, to meet with federal officials, according to project preservation architect Jay Turnbull of Page & Turnbull. "It illustrates that if you have an idea that is strong and push and push and push, eventually you can get it through," said Turnbull.

The building now has forty-six shops, restaurants, and cafes. Ian Garrone of the Marin-based mushroom producer Far West Fungi said they were shocked when Ferry Building management approached them about opening a store there. They had booths in plenty of farmers markets. But an actual store? "The concept of mushrooms as a one-product store—well, I don't think it would work anywhere else," he said.

BUILT: 1898

AWARDED: 2004

OWNER: Equity Office, Port of San Francisco, Wilson Meany Sullivan

ORIGINAL ARCHITECT: A. Page Brown

LEAD ARCHITECT: SMWM, Cathy Simon, FAIA

PRESERVATION ARCHITECT: Page & Turnbull, J. Gordon Turnbull, FAIA

LEAD STRUCTURAL ENGINEER: Rutherford & Chekene, Richard Niewiarowski, Principal-in-Charge

GENERAL CONTRACTOR: Plant Construction Company

GLOBE MILLS SACRAMENTO

IN 1964 AS PILLSBURY prepared to shut down its flour mill on the edge of downtown Sacramento, a worker deep in the bowels of the head house scratched a farewell message on a galvanized storage tank. He wrote: "June 19. Gone With The Wind. Kiss Your Ass Goodbye."

So began a forty-year decline of the mighty Globe Mills complex. What was once the centerpiece of Sacramento's booming food-production industry became a hulking blight. Its main mill building and two dozen seventy-foot concrete silos loomed over the vast Southern Pacific rail yard, attracting squatters and bored teenagers as well as pyromaniacs. Building officials condemned the property and sought to have it knocked down. The property owners wanted nothing to do with the buildings or the $1 million in liens

Above left: Southwest elevation with silos, 2008. Image © Cathy Kelly Photography. *Above right:* Silo staircase, 2008. Image courtesy of M. F. Malinowski, AIA. *Previous page:* Image © 2008 Cathy Kelly Photography.

against the property. In 1996 a three-alarm fire gutted the main mill building. By 2000 it seemed obvious that the derelict mill, like the workers who once populated it, would soon be gone with the wind.

But far from city hall a small handful of persistent outsiders had other ideas. Where city bureaucrats saw a nuisance, architect Michael Malinowski and artist Bruce Boohers saw an "iconic ruin" deserving of a second chance. With no promise of financial reward, the pair spent thousands of hours researching the property and coming up with a plan. They convinced city hall not only to delay demolition but also to allocate $80,000 to stabilize the property.

Malinowski and Boohers then joined forces with Skip Rosenbloom, a physician who was interested in urban-infill development, and Cyrus Youssefi, an experienced affordable-housing developer. Soon they had a project that was approved and financed. "Once you got

Globe Mills loft, 2008. Image © Rich Baum Photography.

bit by the Globe bug, you had to figure out a way to save it," said Malinowski. "There is a brutal honesty about the place."

Turning the mill and silos into homes took not only architectural creativity but also physical sacrifice. For eight hours a day contractors hung in cages from the mill building's five-story ceiling, hacking through the silos' eight-inch-thick concrete sides with hydraulic saws. Shear walls and floors were then poured in place at the height of the original floor plates so the historic window openings could be retained.

Workers repurposed adjacent silos as elevator shafts and stairwells. Dividing walls were poured to form corridors and individual apartments. Old metal funnels became lighting fixtures. Atop the concrete silos is the head house, which was renovated as a residents' lounge. "These weren't buildings in a conventional sense," said Malinowski. "A building is for human occupancy. These were not for human occupancy. This whole site was a machine designed to process grain. Now it's a machine for living."

Today the property includes 114 low-income senior housing units and 31 market-rate lofts. Even more than preserving history, Rosenbloom takes pride in the mill's new use. "A lot of our residents worked their whole lives and now live on social security," he said. "We can't bring back the mills where so many guys lost their livelihood. But in our own small way maybe we are helping by giving people a decent, affordable place to live."

BUILT: 1914

AWARDED: 2009

OWNER: CFY Development, Cyrus Youssefi

ORIGINAL ARCHITECT: P. J. Herold

ARCHITECT: Applied Architecture, Mike Malinowski

STRUCTURAL ENGINEER: Miyamoto International, Inc., Lon Determan

CONSTRUCTION MANAGER: Vanir Construction Management Inc.

Globe Mills community garden, with hundred-year-old wood beams salvaged from the historic barley mill structure, 2008. Image © Cathy Kelly Photography.

FORD ASSEMBLY BUILDING RICHMOND

THE OLD FORD ASSEMBLY Building in Point Richmond is so vital that it's hard to believe it sat empty for fifty years. Today the sawtooth-roofed factory is where Vetrazzo turns recycled glass into kitchen counters. It's where the solar company SunPower designs its latest efficient panels. There, Title Nine sportswear imagines new yoga pants, and Mountain Hardwear creates $700

sleeping bags designed for subzero Himalayan expeditions. Conferences, weddings, and concerts light up the forty-thousand-square-foot Craneway Pavilion, powered by the one-megawatt SunPower solar power plant.

Designed by industrial architecture master Albert Kahn, the Ford Assembly Building rises from the edge

Above left: SunPower conference area, 2008. *Above right:* Administrative level of the SunPower conference area, 2008. Both images © Billy Hustace Photography.

of the bay like the spiky spine of a prehistoric creature. It is a quintessential Kahn daylight factory, a revolutionary design that used a sawtooth roof with ample opaque northern skylights to capture diffused light. The design was an early innovation in green building—workers had plenty of natural light but weren't blasted by direct sun.

The plant opened in August of 1931. On opening day a caravan of Ford's latest models whisked in salesmen from 250 California dealerships. For the next decade it cranked out more Ford Model A's than any plant on the West Coast. In 1942 when the War Production Board halted the manufacturing of civilian cars and trucks, the plant quickly retooled. During the course of World War II the Richmond "Tank Depot" produced forty-nine thousand jeeps and ninety thousand other military vehicles. Surrounded by Richmond's famous "Rosie the Riveter" shipyards, the Ford plant was a central piece of Richmond's mighty wartime military-industrial complex.

After the war, the plant reverted to civilian production, pumping out 325 vehicles a day. But by 1955 Ford decided it needed a bigger plant and closed the Richmond facility in favor of a one-million-square-foot plant near San Jose. Ford held onto the abandoned property until 1979, when the Richmond Community Redevelopment Agency bought it. But for years the building's future didn't look promising. Numerous private developers unsuccessfully tried to take it on. In 1989 the Loma Prieta earthquake shattered thousands of the building's windows and skylights, sheared large sections of brick from the walls, and toppled the brick parapet on the roof.

Finally, in 2005, after trying to buy the property three times, Orton Development acquired it. "A lot of historic buildings don't deserve to be saved," Eddie Orton said at the time. "This is one that actually does." Mark Perrilliat, facilities manager for Mountain Hardwear, recalls sitting on a paint can amid shattered glass and wondering how the building could be brought back to life. "It was a dump," he said.

Today more than one thousand workers toil in the old plant. SunPower's workspace features a central bamboo-clad conference suite and a series of offices overlooking the Craneway. Mountain Hardwear executives sit in the timber-and-glass executive suite that once housed Ford's bigwigs. "This isn't our building, this isn't SunPower's building," said Perrilliat. "It's the city's building."

SunPower offices entrance, 2008. Image © Billy Hustace Photography.

BUILT: 1931

AWARDED: 2009

OWNER: Orton Development, Inc., Eddie Orton

ORIGINAL ARCHITECT: Albert Kahn

ARCHITECT: Marcy Wong Donn Logan Architects, Marcy Wong

PRESERVATION ARCHITECT: Preservation Architecture, Mark Hulbert

STRUCTURAL ENGINEER: The Crosby Group, Ravi Kanitkar

GENERAL CONTRACTOR: Dalzell Corporation, Bruce Hammon

SunPower offices, administrative level, 2008. Image © Billy Hustace Photography.

CAVALLO POINT, THE LODGE AT GOLDEN GATE
SAUSALITO

VETERANS OF THE NINETY-FIRST Division returning to their old stomping grounds at Fort Baker would be in for some surprises. They might not recognize the "contemporary oasis of serenity" that is the Healing Arts Center and Spa at what is now the Cavallo

Point Lodge. The resort's low-key luxury might seem surreal; the US Army was never much for meditation pools, healing sessions with famous shamans, or $35 New York steaks served with poached partridge eggs. Yet perhaps even more of a shock to returning veterans would be how much of Fort Baker's fabric has been preserved, reused, and embraced.

Along with Alcatraz, the Presidio, and Fort Mason, Fort Baker was part of a quartet of forts guarding the Golden Gate. The barracks and other buildings, overlooking the Golden Gate Bridge in Marin County, were constructed between 1902 and 1910 during the so-called Endicott Period, a time when the army was focused on modernizing seacoast forts and improving the living conditions of enlisted soldiers.

For the next ninety years Fort Baker was host to members of the Coast Artillery Corps, the Harbor Defenses of San Francisco, the Sixth Region US Army Air Defense Command, and finally to training support for the Ninety-first Division, a.k.a. the Wild West Division. In 1995 the military transferred its land to Golden Gate National Recreation Area. In 2000 the last soldiers left Fort Baker.

For seven years the town of Sausalito fought a National Park Service's plan to convert the fort into a

Above: Restored exteriors of guest lodging (historic officers' quarters) along the parade ground, 2008. *Opposite:* Front of a historic barracks building with a reconstructed two-story porch, 2008. Both images © David Wakely.

350-room resort. Through political pressure the town finally whittled down the maximum number of rooms to 142. And in the end, it was a battle worth fighting: instead of overwhelming the historic fort, the Park Service embraced it. "It required an extraordinary commitment to stay the course and work to keep the natural beauty in a setting that is almost spiritual in its beauty and serenity," said the late Sausalito mayor Amy Belser, who led the fight to scale down the development.

The original buildings were white clapboard Colonial Revival and, like San Francisco's Presidio, were clustered around a main parade ground. The buildings were large, solid, and symmetrical, with columns, wraparound porches, and wood-sash windows. For the design team, architects Leddy Maytum Stacy and Architectural Resources Group, converting the property to a boutique resort was all about celebrating what the army had left behind.

Overall, the team restored twenty-one historic buildings, saving 97 percent of the exterior envelope and 67 percent of interior surfaces. A chapel and gym were converted to meeting space; concrete bunkers

Left: Original entry lobby and stair retained in guest lodging, 2008. *Right:* Entry and original stair, 2008. Both images © David Wakely.

Typical guest-room interior, 2008. Image © David Wakely.

became a maintenance shed, laundry room, and engineering office. Stamped tin ceilings, which had been shellacked with layer upon layer of white paint, were put in refrigerated cargo containers, which caused the metal to contract and the paint to flake off. Thirteen two-story modern lodging buildings added seventy-four rooms and a new spa.

The heart of the lodge is the wood-frame barracks overlooking the parade ground. The two buildings, home to the lodge's restaurant, bar, art gallery, and gift shop, originally had front porches, but at some point the army had removed them. The restored porches give the place a commons, and direct attention to the Golden Gate Bridge, the sparkling bay, and the bleached-out San Francisco skyline beyond. "The porches are essential to the place now—it's where you sit with the rocking chair and the beer. They face the bridge. They get sun. They are key to the social interaction of the place," said preservation architect Stephen Farneth of Architectural Resources Group.

BUILT: 1902–1910

AWARDED: 2008

ORIGINAL ARCHITECT:
US Army Corps of Engineers

PRINCIPAL: The Fort Baker
Retreat Group, LLC, Tom
Sargent, Principal

ARCHITECT (NEW BUILDINGS):
Leddy Maytum Stacy Architects,
Marsha Maytum, FAIA

ARCHITECT (HISTORIC
BUILDINGS): Architectural
Resources Group, Inc., Stephen
Farneth, FAIA

STRUCTURAL ENGINEER: Murphy
Burr Curry, David Murphy

GENERAL CONTRACTOR: Herrero
Contractors, Inc., Mark Herrero

Restored exteriors of guest lodging (historic officers' quarters) along the parade ground, 2008. Image © David Wakely.

PRESIDIO LANDMARK SAN FRANCISCO

CHRISTINA ARENA LIVES IN San Francisco, but the noises that keep her up at night are not sirens or car alarms but the five-beat hoots of great horned owls. Not that she minds. "Here I am in the middle of a major city with public transportation and access to anything I could possibly need, and I am being kept awake by *owls,*" said Arena.

Arena and her toddler son live in the former merchant-marine hospital on the southern edge of San Francisco's Presidio National Park. Nearly thirty years

Above left: Hospital staircase before renovation, 2006. Image courtesy of Perkins & Will. *Above right*: Restored main lobby. *Previous page*: A new addition atop the rear wing faces two elegantly designed courtyards. Image © www.rickchapman.com/www.birdmaninc.com.

after the last veteran was treated and the facility was shut down, the 1932 Georgian Revival building was reborn in 2010 as a 154-unit apartment community.

Initially, developer Forest City wanted to build a much bigger project—350 units—renovating the military hospital's two 1950s-era wings. But neighbors in the adjacent Inner Richmond pushed for a smaller project, and according to preservation architect Carolyn Kiernat of Page & Turnbull, federal regulators insisted that if the wings were retained, the developer would also

have to keep the one-story addition that had been built right in the middle of the courtyard. "You couldn't see the main entrance if you retained the one-story addition," Kiernat said. "There was a philosophical question of looking at a building that had changed so drastically over time and figuring out if there was a way to bring multiple eras back to life. But they wouldn't let us pick and choose."

The removal of bulky flanks brought into focus the crisp and classical lines of Depression-era design.

Apartment layouts feature high ceilings and extensive natural light. Image © www.rickchapman.com/www.birdmaninc.com.

Suddenly, the seven-story buff brick building was saturated in natural light. Ocean views were freed up. Nestled on the southern edge of the verdant national park, the building became a buffer between the low-scale pastels of the Richmond District and the towering redwoods and eucalyptus of the lush park.

But it wasn't an easy transformation. Forest City replaced twenty thousand bricks to match the original hue, restored eight hundred of the sturdy mahogany windows, and sourced limestone for the facade from the same quarry in Indiana as the original. White paint was scraped off the wainscoting in the staircase and lobby, exposing the light gray Tennessee marble. Construction had to be halted during raptor nesting season.

Project architect Andrew Wolfram of Perkins & Wills said the job was helped by the fact that the army had found it more cost-effective not to demolish original details. For example, bathrooms had been built in front of the original limestone portico. "The government had done the cheapest and most expeditious way, which was not to demolish but to build over," said Wolfram.

Today the building is far removed from its austere military roots, with New York–style doormen, personal wine storage, hot tubs, yoga rooms, newspapers, and fresh coffee in the lobby. But even amid the luxury, one never forgets the building's former use. The web is replete with sites dedicated to the three decades when it was a magnet for graffiti artists and thrill seekers. Ghost stories abound of wounded veterans of past conflicts prowling the hallways. Photographs from that era show monotone prints of Anne Frank pasted onto the building's upper-story windows.

Wolfram said he'd never encountered any of the building's spirits, but that didn't mean he wasn't a bit spooked on occasion. One night he was studying some drawings under a lamp in the basement when he heard something scraping around. He shined a flashlight in the dark corner: it was a raccoon with a Yoplait yogurt container incongruously lodged on its snout.

BUILT: 1932

AWARDED: 2011

OWNER (PUBLIC-PRIVATE PARTNERSHIP): Presidio Trust, Chandler McCoy

ORIGINAL ARCHITECT: US Army Corps of Engineers

DEVELOPER (PUBLIC-PRIVATE PARTNERSHIP): Forest City Development, Alexa Arena

ARCHITECT: Perkins & Will, Andrew Wolfram

PRESERVATION ARCHITECT: Page & Turnbull

STRUCTURAL ENGINEER: Nabih Youssef Associates, Michael Gemmill

GENERAL CONTRACTOR: Plant Construction Company, Craig Allison

The former hospital building, now 154 apartments with amenities, was carefully integrated into the national park. Image © www.rickchapman.com/www.birdmaninc.com.

CHINESE HISTORICAL SOCIETY OF AMERICA MUSEUM
SAN FRANCISCO

A FEW BLOCKS UP Clay Street from Grant Avenue's plastic Buddhas and $9.99 kimonos, the Chinese Historical Society of America is a place most tourists don't venture. It's too bad: the Julia Morgan–designed former YWCA is a rich anthology of Chinese American stories and a monument to the struggles of San Francisco's Chinatown.

The CHSA opened its doors at 965 Clay Street in 2001, twelve years after damage from the Loma Prieta earthquake forced the YWCA to vacate the building. With a $1.4 million budget, architect Barcelon & Jang revived the building as a boutique museum while preserving Julia Morgan's mix of Chinese cultural motifs and Western Arts and Crafts style. The main gym became a gem of an exhibit hall lit with subtle wire-suspended lights affording uninterrupted views of Morgan's unusual wood lamella trusses. A clear glass wall converted the old stage into a climate-controlled

Above left: Image courtesy of Barcelon & Jang. *Above right:* The water fountain was repaired in the restored garden court, 2002. Image © Michael H. Ikeda. *Previous page:* In the garden court gallery's interior arcade, the wood trusses were cleaned, the columns were repaired and repainted to match the original colors, and the original painted dragon motif on the cement floor was restored, 2002. Image © Michael H. Ikeda.

gallery. Restored and brought up to code were the building's three Chinese-style towers, its ceramic roof tiles, and its serene courtyard flanked by a glass-walled corridor.

While exhibits evoke hundreds of years of Chinese American history, it is the building itself that best illustrates the plights and triumphs of the Chinese experience in San Francisco. The Chinatown YWCA organization was founded in 1916 to "associate Chinese women and girls in Christian fellowship." But the building the

organization was housed in, a dingy former saloon on Sacramento Street, was hardly conducive to fellowship. So it was a bit disconcerting in 1930 for neighborhood women to learn that the YWCA was putting up a new center at 940 Powell Street, literally fifty steps beyond what was then considered Chinatown's border. The notion that this new building would be so close to Chinatown yet off-limits to Chinese American women in still-segregated California, provoked a powerful reaction. Chinatown YWCA members demanded a

The gymnasium was transformed into an exhibition space for documenting the history of Chinese people in America, 2002. Image © Michael H. Ikeda.

new building of their own; the YWCA responded with a compromise: they would build one on Clay Street, but the Chinese American community had to pay for it.

The women of Chinatown did it, raising $25,000 during the depth of the Depression. Today, the old Y remains a special place for Chinatown natives. Nolan Chow, who works at the museum front desk, says his first memories were of napping on the gym floor under Julia Morgan's vaulted ceiling. Others remember climbing up Clay Street on chilly winter evenings in tutus and hearing the "one, two...now lift" of ballet instruction. A photograph of Chinatown teens registering voters in the 1970s brought back other memories. "That boy holding the pen is Bayard Fong," wrote one woman. "Is that girl in the photo Joanna Louie?"

BUILT: 1932

AWARDED: 2005

ORIGINAL ARCHITECT:
Julia Morgan

EXECUTIVE DIRECTOR:
CHSA, Sue Lee

PRINCIPAL: Barcelon & Jang Architecture, Wayne Barcelon, AIA, and Darlene Jang, AIA

LEAD ENGINEER: KYA & Associates, Kam Yan, SE

GENERAL CONTRACTOR:
Transworld Construction, Inc., Geomen Liu

The original 1931 exterior brick facade, copper barrel roof, crenellated glazed tiles, and deep-set windows were preserved and restored, 2001. Image © Michael H. Ikeda.

JAPANESE AMERICAN NATIONAL MUSEUM
LOS ANGELES

THE ORIGINAL NISHI HONGWANJI Buddhist Temple in Little Tokyo is a testament to the strength and resilience of Los Angeles's Japanese American community. Somehow it survived the internment of Japanese Americans during World War II, a tenure as a Baptist church, a few ill-conceived urban renewal efforts, and finally the 1994 Northridge earthquake. Today the temple, part of the Japanese American National Museum complex, sits in the center of a Little Tokyo cultural district that has blossomed as part of L.A.'s broader downtown revival.

The brick temple was completed in 1925 on the site of a former pool hall, part of a lively commercial strip along First Street. It was the heart of the Japanese American community, home to everything from weddings to funerals to movies and concerts. Partly,

Above left: Front entrance, 1993. *Above right:* Interior stairwell, 1992. *Previous page:* View from the balcony of the Hirasaki Family Gallery, 1993. All images courtesy of James R. McElwain, AIA.

the temple-as-social-center developed as a response to American Christian-centric culture. Sunday church service was the epicenter of community life in many neighborhoods, and if the temple wanted to prevent defections to Christian churches, it would have to create a Buddhist alternative to the Sunday service. "That to me is a perfect example of what it means to be Japanese American—that something new was created out of two different traditions," said Chris Komai, a local historian whose family owned the neighborhood newspaper.

When Japanese Americans were forced into internment during World War II, the temple became a warehouse for the possessions and furniture left behind.

The Reverend Julius Goldwater, an American convert to Buddhism and ordained Buddhist priest, watched over the temple and its members' possessions until they were released. As the only priest in the local Buddhist diocese who was not of Japanese ancestry, he assumed responsibility for all the temples in the district. Goldwater was later dismissive about what he had done. "I only behaved as any American would have done," he told the *Los Angeles Daily News* in 1992.

In the late 1960s, city officials informed the temple of plans to add additional lanes of traffic to First Street, essentially wiping out the historic center of Little Tokyo. The temple was proactive, and in 1969 the congregation moved to a new facility a block over, at 815 East First Street. The city never followed through on its redevelopment scheme, and for twenty years the original building sat empty.

Finally, in 1986 the city, which had taken possession of the property, agreed to lease it to the Japanese American National Museum. During a $13 million restoration, the temple was strengthened and brought up to seismic standards. Lotus stencils were repaired and repainted. Wood banisters and theater seats were restored. Eventually, the museum built a new eighty-five-thousand-square-foot modern building and now owns both, with a courtyard between them.

Today much of the original temple building is dedicated to the National Center for the Preservation of Democracy, which promotes the principles of democracy, diversity, and civic engagement. In the former temple, students learn about the Japanese American 442nd Regimental Combat Team and other groups that fought in segregated units during World War II. "We never wanted this building to be abandoned or closed," said Komai. "So much history is here."

BUILT: 1925

AWARDED: 1993

OWNER: Japanese American National Museum

ORIGINAL ARCHITECT: Edgar Cline

ARCHITECT: KNSU Joint Venture Architects

PRESERVATION ARCHITECT: James R. McElwain, AIA

GENERAL CONTRACTOR: Plant Construction Company

The Legacy Center, 1992. Image courtesy of James R. McElwain, AIA.

ALTENHEIM SENIOR HOUSING OAKLAND

IF A COMMUNITY CAN be judged by how well it cares for its elderly, Bay Area German Americans scored high marks in the late nineteenth century.

In May of 1890, San Francisco's German American leaders convened a meeting to address a growing concern: how to create a home where aged men and women could live out their *Lebensabend*—old age—in peace and dignity. The group, which included San Francisco Mayor Adolph Sutro, banker Mortimer Fleishhacker, and stained-glass merchant Fritz Rosenbaum, looked on both sides of the bay for the perfect location. After deeming San Francisco too foggy and cool, the group paid $6,000 for a hilltop parcel in Oakland's Dimond District, a German American enclave overlooking Friedrich Rhoda's cherry orchards, Charlie Schumacher's fruit trees, and the *Biergartens* of Trepper and Bauerhofer.

Here the group built a castle that spilled out onto a six-acre maze of flower gardens and walking paths. The home—named Altenheim, which is German for retirement home—survived the great earthquake of 1906 but burned down in 1908. A new building was reconstructed, with occupancy starting again in October 1909. For more than eighty years the building served its purpose as a retirement home and German cultural center. But the number of German American residents gradually dwindled, and the cost of running the historic home became prohibitive. In 2002 it went out of business.

Independent schools and condo developers went after the property, but eventually the Altenheim board determined that affordable senior housing was the best use. A deal was reached in which the Citizens Housing

Above: South porches, 2007. *Opposite:* Solarium, 2007. Both images © Frank Domin.

Corporation (later taken over by Eden Housing) would convert the home to ninety apartments and develop an additional eighty units on another parcel. The Altenheim preserved another building on the property as a German language school and cultural center.

Citizens Housing restored the estate's brick raised basement, Doric columns, and expansive porches. Today visitors are ushered into a formal entrance with a domed skylight punctured by an oculus. The original donors are listed on one wall, and a grandfather clock brought from Germany in 1911 chimes the hour.

Another part of the restoration project, the Craftsman dining hall where German opera is still performed on New Year's Day, feels rustic with its exposed timber trusses and beams.

During the renovation the Altenheim board members took turns sleeping in the building. "We all know what happens to historic buildings that are left vacant—they are stripped in about ten minutes," said architect Michael Willis, who sits on the board. "We made sure that building was never dark, not one single night."

Left: Main entry rotunda, 2007. *Right:* Dining room, 2007. Both images © Frank Domin.

Today, the property houses about 150 seniors of modest means. The residents represent a wide range of ethnic backgrounds and work side by side in the community garden. Wei Guang Wu, a retired seventy-one-year-old herbalist who moved to the United States from China six years ago, plants melons, bok choy, and Chinese broccoli. Nearby, Erka Benbow—one of the few German-born residents—favors fava beans, shallots, and tomatoes. "I walked the grounds and I counted more than 175 species of plant, flower, and tree," Benbow said. "In some instances I knew the English names, sometimes I knew the German. Sometimes both."

BUILT: 1909

AWARDED: 2007

ORIGINAL ARCHITECT: Charles Mau

PRESIDENT: Citizens Housing Corporation, Jim Buckley

SENIOR PROJECT MANAGER: Citizens Housing Corporation, Kaori Tokunaga

ARCHITECT, PRINCIPAL-IN-CHARGE: Pyatok Architects, Inc., Elizabeth Yost, AIA

ASSOCIATED ARCHITECT: Alan Dreyfuss Architects, Alan Dreyfuss, AIA

PRESERVATION ARCHITECT: Architectural Resources Group, Inc., Naomi O. Miroglio

SENIOR PRINCIPAL PROJECT ENGINEER, STRUCTURAL: Degenkolb Engineers, Loring Wyllie Jr. and Arne Halterman

LANDSCAPE ARCHITECT: PGAdesign, Cathy Garrett, ASLA, LEED AP, and Chris Pattillo, ASLA

GENERAL CONTRACTOR: Swinerton Builders, Kevin Shiplett, Project Engineer

East porch, 2007. Image © Frank Domin.

USS HORNET MUSEUM ALAMEDA

ON JULY 24, 1969, when the Apollo 11 mission splashed into the Pacific Ocean 860 miles west of Hawaii, the USS *Hornet* was waiting just fifty miles to the south. With President Nixon on board, the aircraft carrier fished astronauts Neil Armstrong, Edwin "Buzz" Aldrin, and Michael Collins from the sea, welcoming them back to planet Earth. Photographs taken that day show Nixon laughing as he converses with the three blue-uniformed astronauts through the window of a special quarantine room the astronauts lived in for three weeks upon their return. "This is the greatest week in the history of the world," Nixon told the astronauts. "As a result of what you've done, the world has never been closer together before."

The recovery of the astronauts was perhaps the most famous mission of the USS *Hornet*—but it was certainly not the first time the aircraft carrier had made history. Built in Newport News, Virginia, and launched in 1943, the Essex Class USS *Hornet* CV-12 aircraft carrier was part of the buildup of the nation's carrier force during World War II. Wasp-waisted and flat-topped, the aircraft carrier is a behemoth. She once carried 107 planes and was home to 3,500 men. She weighs 41,600 tons and stretches the length of three football fields. The

top of her mast rises 193 feet in the air. Each link of her anchor chain weighs 120 pounds.

The *Hornet* holds the record for the number of enemy planes its pilots downed in the Pacific theater in World War II. She played a central role in several of the heaviest and most critical battles in the Pacific, earning seven battle stars and a Presidential Unit Citation. The carrier was home to Lieutenant Colonel James Doolittle, an Alameda native and one of the most decorated pilots in US history. On April 18, 1942, Doolittle

Above left: The *Hornet's* island before restoration. Image courtesy of the USS Hornet Museum Archives. *Above right:* Present-day view of the *Hornet's* island. Image © Carol Lee, USS Hornet Museum. *Previous page:* Restored USS *Hornet*. Image © Bob Fish.

led a mission of sixteen B-25 bombers above Tokyo, Nagoya, and Yokohama that sent Japan a clear message of American airpower.

Mothballed in 1970, the *Hornet* sat fallow until 1995 when the navy sold it for scrap for $188,000. The idea that the mighty ship would be sold off as scrap metal mobilized former crew members, who formed a foundation to save her. From mid-1995 to May 1998 the group raised startup funds and worked successfully to save the USS *Hornet*. After completing cleanup tasks such as asbestos removal, foam and lead paint strip-

ping, and fire-safety improvements, the crew started restoration of the chief spaces to accommodate visitors and staff. The long-term goal was to restore all of the superstructure and hangar deck, putting the ship into "near operable condition."

The USS Hornet Museum officially opened her hatches to the public in October 1998. Today the museum holds events to make sure the exploits of the *Hornet*—and US military history more broadly—are remembered. On Memorial Day in 2011 the Young American Patriots Fife and Drum Corps performed,

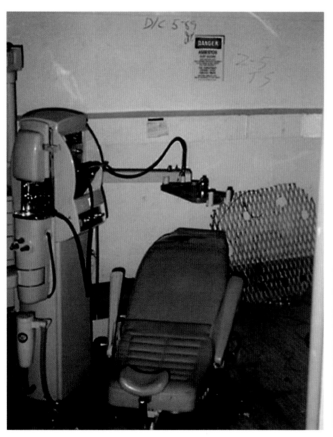 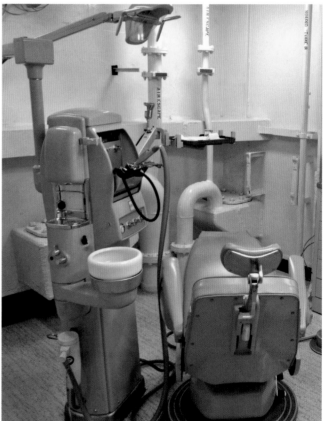

Left: One of four examination rooms before restoration. Image courtesy of the USS Hornet Museum Archives. *Right*: An examination room after complete restoration. Image © Carol Lee, USS Hornet Museum.

as well as the USS Hornet Band. Afterward, flowers were tossed from the edge of the *Hornet* as a bugler played taps and the petals floated away in the San Francisco Bay. In 2012 veterans and history buffs gathered to honor the late Lieutenant Doolittle. Granddaughter Jonna Doolittle Hoppes urged the audience to preserve the stories that are dying off with the veterans that lived them. "I look around this room and I feel my grandfather's story is no more important than every story in this room," she said. "If we don't find a way to record these stories, our history, it is going to be lost."

BUILT: 1943

AWARDED: 2004

OWNER: USS Hornet Museum

ORIGINAL ARCHITECT: Unknown

PROJECT LEAD: USS Hornet Museum, Ralph Johnson, Chief Operating Officer

PRESERVATION ARCHITECT: US Navy

SPONSOR: Alameda Architectural Preservation Society

Present-day Hangar Bay 3. Image © Carol Lee, USS Hornet Museum.

ABOUT THE AUTHORS

J. K. DINEEN writes about urban planning and architecture for the *San Francisco Business Times.* He has been a staff writer at the *San Francisco Examiner,* the *New York Daily News,* and a variety of daily and weekly newspapers in his native Massachusetts. His work has also appeared in the *New York Observer* and *Travel & Leisure.* He lives in San Francisco with his wife, Megan Fletcher, and children, Amelia and Patrick.

JOHN KING is the *San Francisco Chronicle's* urban design critic and the author of *Cityscapes.* He joined the paper in 1992 and has been in his current post since 2001. His writing on architecture and urban design has been honored by groups including the California Preservation Foundation, the Society of Professional Journalists, and the California chapters of the American Institute of Architects and the American Planning Association. He was a finalist for the Pulitzer Prize for Criticism in 2002 and 2003.

HEYDAY
into California

ABOUT HEYDAY

Heyday is an independent, nonprofit publisher and unique cultural institution. We promote widespread awareness and celebration of California's many cultures, landscapes, and boundary-breaking ideas. Through our well-crafted books, public events, and innovative outreach programs we are building a vibrant community of readers, writers, and thinkers.

THANK YOU

It takes the collective effort of many to create a thriving literary culture. We are thankful to all the thoughtful people we have the privilege to engage with. Cheers to our writers, artists, editors, storytellers, designers, printers, bookstores, critics, cultural organizations, readers, and book lovers everywhere!

We are especially grateful for the generous funding we've received for our publications and programs during the past year from foundations and hundreds of individual donors. Major supporters include:

Anonymous (3); Acorn Naturalists; Alliance for California Traditional Arts; Arkay Foundation; Judy Avery; James J. Baechle; Paul Bancroft III; BayTree Fund; S. D. Bechtel, Jr. Foundation; Barbara Jean and Fred Berensmeier; Berkeley Civic Arts Program and Civic Arts Commission; Joan Berman; Buena Vista Rancheria/Jesse Flyingcloud Pope Foundation; John Briscoe; Lewis and Sheana Butler; California Civil Liberties Public Education Program; Cal Humanities; California Indian Heritage Center Foundation; California State Library; California State Parks Foundation; Keith Campbell Foundation; Candelaria Fund; John and Nancy Cassidy Family Foundation, through Silicon Valley Community Foundation; The Center for California Studies; Charles Edwin Chase; Graham Chisholm; The Christensen Fund; Jon Christensen; Community Futures Collective; Compton Foundation; Creative Work Fund; Lawrence Crooks; Nik Dehejia; Frances Dinkelspiel and Gary Wayne; The Durfee Foundation; Earth Island Institute; Eaton Kenyon Fund of the Sacramento Region Community Foundation; Euclid Fund at the East Bay Community Foundation; Foothill Resources, Ltd.; Furthur Foundation; The Fred Gellert Family Foundation; Fulfillco;

GETTING INVOLVED
To learn more about our publications, events, membership club, and other ways you can participate, please visit www.heydaybooks.com.